CHRISTIANITY
AND
CIVILISATION

By
EMIL BRUNNER

FIRST PART :
FOUNDATIONS

GIFFORD LECTURES DELIVERED AT
THE UNIVERSITY OF ST. ANDREWS
1947

CHARLES SCRIBNER'S SONS
New York · 1948

PREFACE

NEVER, when about to publish a book, have I experienced such a conflict of feeling as I have in laying before the public this first series of Gifford Lectures, delivered in the University of St. Andrews in February and March, 1947. On the one hand, for many years I have been convinced that such an attempt at a Christian doctrine of the foundations of civilisation is overdue, having regard in particular to the situation and the responsibility of the Protestant churches. It really ought to have been made long ago. What might not have been avoided if it had! Sometimes I even think it is already too late. At any rate, if by the mercy of God we are to have some further breathing space, if He does grant us another chance to build up a new European civilisation on the ruins of the old, facing all the time the possibility of an imminent end to all civilised life on this globe, Christianity has a tremendous responsibility.

In this book I seek to formulate and to justify my conviction that only Christianity is capable of furnishing the basis of a civilisation which can rightly be described as human. It is obvious that a clear conception of the relation between Christianity and civilisation in their different spheres is of paramount importance for such a task. Therefore somebody has to begin, however inadequate may be his resources compared with the immensity and difficulty of the work to be done.

It is this feeling of inescapable urgency which has prompted me to hasten the publication of my first series of lectures, which deal with the fundamental presuppositions. I should hardly have overcome my hesitation, however, had I not received so much spontaneous encouragement from my hearers, particularly from my colleagues on the staff of the University of St. Andrews, who appeared to be unanimously of the opinion that this initial series should be published without delay.

On the other hand, the more I considered the problem as a whole, the more alarmed I was by the disproportion between its vastness and the incompleteness of my equipment for dealing with it. Whilst I am fully confident and free from anxiety in my own mind as to my main theses, I have little doubt that the detail of my argument, particularly in its historical sections, presents many openings for criticism, whether by the expert in the history of philosophy, or the historian of civilisation. As the lay-out of my lectures is topical or systematic, and not historical, it was unavoidable that each chapter should somehow follow the whole course of European history, and that, necessarily, in seven league boots. The historian is entitled to dislike such surveys which cannot do justice to the manifold aspects and facts of historical reality. Simplifications are necessary in all sciences; one might even say that simplification is the very essence of science. But over-simplifications may be unjustifiable from various points of view. On some of these I am not too sure that I shall not be found at fault.

Furthermore, I feel most vividly the disproportion between the magnitude of each of the main topics I am dealing with and the brevity and sketchiness of their treatment in a number of chapters, each the length of an hour's discourse. From the point of view of the scholar, it would have been preferable to choose one of them only and try to treat it more or less exhaustively. But then the main purpose, which was exactly the opposite—namely to show under a variety of aspects the same fundamental dependence of our civilisation on its Christian basis—would have been defeated. I therefore hope that my readers will bear in mind this main purpose and make allowance for the inevitable limitations resulting from it.

There are, it seems to me, two kinds of scientific conscientiousness, the one demanding specialisation with all its inherent possibilities of profundity, the other calling for a venture in synthesis with all its danger of superficiality. The European mind of the last century has been developed so entirely and exclusively along the first line, that any attempt at synthesis is looked upon as a sign of arrogance and as irresponsible dilettantism. But there are times—and such a time is ours—when synthesis must be risked, whatever the cost. Perhaps the one who so ventures has to pay the penalty and accept without grumbling the reproach of unscientific, premature audacity. Still, I cannot quite suppress the hope that there may be some, even amongst those with high standards of scientific probity, who can see that it is not lack of respect for their standards, or youthful impertinence, but a feeling of imperative necessity which might prompt such an undertaking. Having already published not a few extensive monographs, I may be entitled to hope that this plea will not be misunderstood.

The specific character of the topic of these lectures, which makes necessary such a venture in synthesis, may be accepted also as justification for the fact that the " scientific apparatus ", which in my previous books has been rather too heavy, is this time very slight. The field covered in this book is so vast that complete documentation is altogether impossible, so that it seemed to me more honest not to attempt it.

May I conclude this preface with an expression of my deepest gratitude to the Senate of the University of St. Andrews for the great honour they have shown me in inviting me to give this course of Gifford Lectures, and for the extraordinary kindness and friendliness with which the members of the staff, particularly of the Theological Faculty, received me and made me feel at home in their delightful and historic town.

E. B.

CONTENTS

CHRISTIANITY AND CIVILISATION

FIRST SERIES: THE FOUNDATIONS

I

THE PROBLEM OF A CHRISTIAN CIVILISATION

SINCE Mr. Churchill at a historic hour spoke words which
have themselves made history about the survival of Christian civilisation, the idea of Christian civilisation and its
being endangered in the highest degree has become familiar
among the Western nations. We have become conscious of the
fact that in the course of some fifteen centuries something like a
Christian civilisation has been created, and of the other fact
that in our days this Christian civilisation is at stake and its
survival is questioned. Mr. Churchill's warning has retained
its full actuality even now, after the battle of Britain has ended
in victory. For, unfortunately, the pressures to which the
foundations of this culture were exposed, have not decreased
since then, but rather increased. It is necessary to remember,
however, that this danger must have been acute for some time
in the past. Before the world had heard the name Adolf Hitler,
a solitary thinker, unknown till then, Oswald Spengler by name,
had written a startling book with the almost apocalyptic title,
Der Untergang des Abendlandes [1]. His ominous prophecy
of the end of Western cultural tradition, based on his analysis
of European history of the last centuries, is to be interpreted as
meaning that the time is past when spiritual forces and values
determine the face and character of the Western world. A new
epoch has begun, in which the scholar, the artist, the seer and
the saint are replaced by the soldier, the engineer and the man of
political power; an epoch which is no more capable of producing
real culture, but merely an outward technical civilisation. But

even Spengler was not the first to utter such dismal ideas about the future.

Fifty years before Spengler, the great Swiss historian, Jakob Burckhardt, who fifty years after his death is being more and more universally considered as the greatest continental interpreter of the history of civilisation, had sketched a picture of the future of the Western world which is not less terrifying.[2]   This picture, like that of Spengler, is dominated by the figure of the political military dictator, gaining and sustaining his position by means of mass-psychology and extirpating all spiritual culture by his brutal militarism and imperialism.   What then was seen by such prophetic minds as a terrible future, has become meanwhile an even more gloomy reality, although, thank God, until now merely a partial reality.

The mere fact that more than half a century ago a man, thoroughly awake to the character of his time, was able to foresee the catastrophe we have experienced, indicates that the eruption of inhumanity, lawlessness and depersonalisation, which we have experienced during recent decades, must have had its deep historical roots.   True, this eruption of anti-spiritual and anti-cultural forces, as they appeared first in the Bolshevist, then in the Fascist, and finally in the National-Socialist revolution, came to the rest of the Western world as a complete surprise and left it in utter bewilderment.   Still, looking back on these events, this feeling of complete surprise and horror is not altogether justified in view of the fact that the spiritual evolution during the last centuries was a slow and invisible, but none the less indubitable preparation for this outbreak.   If we ask, as certainly many during these years have asked, how all this, this inhumanity, this lawlessness, this collectivist depersonalisation, was possible, the answer cannot, I think, be in doubt.   The last three centuries, seen from the spiritual point of view, represent a history in which step by step the central and fundamental idea of the whole Western civilisation, the idea of the dignity of man, was undermined and weakened.[3]   For more than a thousand years Western culture had been based on the Christian idea that man is created in the image of God.   This central

Biblical idea included both the eternal spiritual destiny of every individual and the destiny of mankind to form a free communion. With the Enlightenment, this idea, on which the whole structure of Western life was rested, began to be doubted.

At first the alternative to the Christian idea was still a religious, although no longer distinctly Christian, theism. Then, further from the Christian foundation, there came a transcendentalism or idealism, which still remained metaphysical, although no longer explicitly theistic. In the middle of the last century this idealistic humanism was replaced by a positivist philosophy of freedom and civilisation, which acknowledged no metaphysical but merely natural presuppositions. It is not surprising that this positivism in its turn more and more lost its humanistic contents and turned into a naturalistic philosophy, for which man was no more than a highly developed animal, the cerebral animal, and this was a conception of man within which such things as the dignity of man, the rights of man, and personality no longer had any foundation. Benjamin Constant, that noble Christian philosopher of freedom of the early 19th century, has comprehended the essence of this whole process of modern history in three words: " De la divinité par l'humanité à la bestialité ". The totalitarian revolutions, with their practice of inhumanity, lawlessness and depersonalising collectivism, were nothing but the executors of this so-called positivist philosophy, which, as a matter of fact, was a latent nihilism, and which, towards the end of the last and the beginning of this century, had become the ruling philosophy of our universities and the dominating factor within the world-view of the educated and the leading strata of society. The postulatory atheism of arl Marx and the passionate antitheism of Friedrich Nietzsche be considered as an immediate spiritual presupposition of otalitarian revolution in Bolshevism on the one hand and nal-Socialism or Fascism on the other. That is to say, the nt philosophy of the Occident had become more or less ic.[4] No wonder that from this seed that harvest sprang ch our generation reaped with blood and tears, to use ore Mr. Churchill's words.

This sketch of the spiritual history of the last centuries is admittedly a forced simplification of reality, but why should it not be? It will suffice if, notwithstanding its onesidedness, it expresses something essential. I personally should claim that it does more: it does not merely express something essential, but the essential. Taken as a whole, the Western world has moved in this direction, away from a Christian starting point towards a naturalistic and therefore nihilistic goal, an evolution which could not but end in the totalitarian revolutions and the formation of totalitarian states, of which one of the most powerful has emerged victorious from the battle. The crisis of Western civilisation, which became a life-and-death issue in the fight with National-Socialism, and which is still a life-and-death issue, primarily in view of the victorious totalitarian power in the East, is therefore at bottom a religious crisis. Western civilisation is, according to Mr. Churchill's word, a Christian civilisation, whatever that may mean. Therefore the progressive estrangement from Christianity, which characterises the history of the last centuries and our time, must necessarily mean a fundamental crisis for this whole civilisation. This crisis at bottom is nothing but a consequence of the fact that the deepest foundation of this civilisation, the Christian faith, has been shaken in the consciousness of European and American nations, and in some parts of this world has been more than shaken, in fact shattered and even annihilated.

This negative thesis has as its presupposition a positive one, which lies in the concept of a Christian civilisation, namely that in some indefinite, but very real sense, Western civilisation wa Christian, and, in so far as it still exists, is Christian. It is mo pleasant to give the proof or justification for this positive th than that for the first negative one, although the two postu each other. Questionable as may be, from the point of vi Christian faith, any bold and uncritical use of the word tian culture, no one who knows our history can deny th contribution of Christianity towards the treasury of a spe Occidental culture has been enormous. Certainly we beware of the illusion that there ever was a Christian

If you understand the word Christian in its full meaning as incorporated in the New Testament, the true disciples of Jesus Christ, as the apostolic teaching presupposes them, were a minority in all centuries of European history and within the Western world at large. But it is just a manifestation of the superhuman power and reality of Christian faith and of the New Testament message, that they are powerful factors within the cultural world, even where life has been only superficially touched by them, or where they are present in very diluted and impure manifestations.

It is this which imposes itself as a manifest fact for every one who studies the cultural history of the West: it is not only the Romanesque and Gothic cathedrals dominating the silhouette of many European cities, not only the frescoes of Fra Angelico in San Marco and of Michelangelo in the Sistine, not only Milton's *Paradise Lost*, Rembrandt's engravings of Biblical stories, Bach's passion according to Saint Matthew, which are unthinkable without the Bible, and without the Church translating, conserving and promulgating this Bible. Our democratic state-forms, also our public and private charitable institutions, the colleges of English and American universities, a multitude of the most important concepts of our psychological, philosophical, juridical and cultural language are directly or indirectly products of Christian tradition and of Christian thinking, feeling and purposing. It was not for nothing that during many centuries the Christian Church had the monopoly of education and instruction, that the invention of the printing press primarily contributed to the spreading of the Bible, that for many centuries the most famous institutions of higher learning were foundations of Christian communities and Churches and were primarily destined for the promotion of Christian knowledge. All that is easily understood if we consider that up to the 19th century every European individual was baptised and instructed by the Christian Church, that furthermore, at least in a superficial sense, the contents of the Bible message were believed by almost everybody and shaped their judgment of what is true and false, good and evil, desirable and undesirable. Certainly there were always some sceptics, doubters, heretics. But they could not manifest themselves as such. Certainly there was, probably in all ages, a large majority of indifferent and lukewarm nominal Christians; but even they stood in an unbroken tradition of doctrine and faith, and even their conscience was formed by the commandments of the Bible, whether they acted according to their conscience or not. Even towards the end of the 18th century, the typical thought of the Enlightenment, with its negative or doubting attitude, was confined to a decided minority within the higher ranks of society. The masses, even the large majority of educated men and women, always thought in the categories of Biblical Christian tradition, however diluted or mis-shaped and distorted the Gospel may have been in this tradition. It is therefore self-evident that in such a world of nations civilisation was deeply imbued, determined and guided by Christian faith, its contents, its norms, its concepts of value. The history of civilisation, as Christian, has not yet been written. What can be grasped of this history, however, by every one who has any knowledge of it and who has any share in European culture, is sufficient to justify that catch-word, " The Christian civilisation of the West ", at least in the sense of an undeniable fact, however different may be the interpretations of this fact.

It seems necessary to me, however, to indicate even in this introductory survey of the field not only the facts, which may be summarised by the phrase, Christian civilisation, but also the deep and bewildering problem which is included in this formula. How questionable the concept of a Christian civilisation is, can be seen from two sides, from that of Christian faith and that of civilisation. Let me start with the first: anyone who approaches the New Testament with the intention of getting instruction about the relation between Christian faith or doctrine and civilisation or culture from the most authoritative source, cannot fail to be astonished, bewildered and even disappointed.[5] Neither the Gospels nor the letters of the apostles, neither the teaching of Jesus himself, nor that of his disciples, seem to encourage us in any way to investigate this relation. Jesus teaches about the kingdom of God and its righteousness, about its coming, its essence and the conditions of the partaking in it, in a way which does not seem to betray any interest in any of those things which we include under the terms civilisation or culture. Quite the contrary. Not only is His own mind unambiguously, not to say onesidedly, directed towards the one goal which—however it may be expressed—is something totally different from what we understand by civilisation; He also requires from His disciples the same unambiguous, uncompromising attitude and orientation. It is true that in the last century the teaching of Jesus about the kingdom of God was often interpreted in a manner which had greater kinship with our social and cultural problems. But this is past. All New Testament scholars nowadays would admit[6] that this 19th century interpretation, whether we like it or not, was a falsification of the historical facts. Whether you understand the kingdom of God more as a present reality or as something to come, in either case it is a reality which entirely transcends the sphere of civilisation. Its content is the ἔσχατον, the ultimate and absolute, the perfect, the truly divine, distinguished from all human relativity. This Gospel is concerned with man's relation to God in its innermost mystery and with the relation to man in the most personal and intimate sense, without any reference to cultural values and social institutions. The teaching of this kingdom of God, however, is the be-all and the end-all of the Gospel of Jesus; there is no room in it for anything else, for all these important but temporal and secular things like art, education, science, social and political order. How then should it be possible for anyone who takes his standards for Christian truth from this Gospel of Jesus, to attempt anything like a Christian doctrine of civilisation?

No more encouraging is the picture which we find in the letters of the apostles, not to speak of that understanding of Christian life and faith which the last book of the Bible, the Apocalypse of John, expresses. It is no more explicitly the proclamation of the kingdom of God which focusses the thoughts and feelings of Christians, but the preaching of salvation, of eternal life in Jesus Christ, of the consummation of all things in the παρουσία of Christ, the Gospel of forgiveness of sins, of redemption, of the divine judgment, of the working of the Holy Spirit in the hearts of the faithful and in the Christian community. It is the proclamation of Resurrection, of the coming final judgment, of the restoration and perfection of all things beyond their historical existence. What has all this to do with the problems and tasks of cultural life? At any rate they never become explicit topics of doctrine. There are a few exceptions to this rule, a few short, although very important, comments on the state, on marriage and family, on the relation between parents and children, masters and slaves, but this is about all. And if you take the last mentioned, the problem of slavery, disappointment becomes even greater; for nothing is said about slavery being an institution which contradicts the principle of human dignity and freedom. On the contrary, we find there an exhortation to the slaves to be satisfied with their lot and loyally to obey their masters. Therefore the result of this investigation seems to be entirely negative with regard to a Christian doctrine of civilisation, whether you attribute this fact to indifference, to the expectation of an imminent end of the world, or to some other cause.

A similar result seems to be gained if you view the relation of Christianity and civilisation from the other side, from that of civilisation. When we survey the history of civilisation before the entrance of Christianity into world history, we have to admit, if we want to be fair, that the civilisation of the pre-Christian era does not seem to lack an essential element which would be introduced only by Christianity. Civilisation and culture seem to live entirely out of their own resources. Who would deny the grandeur of the old Egyptian, Indian or Chinese civilisations? These nations had a magnificent art, excellent institutions of law and state, splendid systems of education and fine culture without any knowledge of God's revelation in Christ or of the teaching of the prophets in the Old Testament. And what about the classical people of the highest culture, the Greeks? Have the achievements of ancient Greece in architecture or sculpture, in epic, lyric or dramatic poetry ever and anywhere been surpassed? Is there in any later epoch anything comparable to the intensity and universality of the Greek scientific mind? Has there ever been, to give one name only, a man comparable to Aristotle, who could claim to have created and mastered so many different branches of science and led them on in that first impetus to the highest level of classical perfection? Or we may think of those cultural values which are less visible. Have the Greeks been surpassed by any later generation in the development of fine manners, of forms of spirited sociability, of that humanism which is sensitive to every noble thing? Is not that same Athens, which produced the Parthenon and Greek tragedy, also the cradle of the oldest democracy of the world? Must not the philosophers of all later generations first become students of Parmenides, Plato and Aristotle and remain within their school all their lives, if they are to produce something worth while? And all that, hundreds of years before Jesus Christ!

This fact confused the first Christian theologians and led them to put forward the hypothesis that the Greek philosophers had learned the best of their philosophy from Moses and the prophets of Israel by some unknown historical mediation. We know to-day that this is not so; we have to content ourselves with the fact, that the highest summit of culture and civilisation which history knows, developed without any influence of Biblical revelation, and we shall have to keep this fact before our eyes whenever we speak about the relation of Christianity and civilisation.[7]

If now we put together these two results of our consideration, on the one hand the intimate connection between Christianity and civilisation in Western history, and the fundamental importance of Christianity for our civilisation, and on the other, the mutual independence and indifference of Christianity and civilisation as it appears from the New Testament as well as from pre-Christian history, the problem of Christian civilisation is intensified and deepened in a way that makes anything like a cheap solution appear completely impossible. So much is clear from the start, that the synthesis included in the concept of a Christian civilisation is full of problems and that this expression

must be used with the greatest caution. From the very outset
we are then in the situation of Socrates: we know that we do not
know what a Christian civilisation is and can be. We know
that we do not have in our hands a ready-made programme
which has simply to be applied.

To be sure, the practical task indicated in Mr. Churchill's
words about the preservation of Christian civilisation exists
and claims supreme attention and effort. All Europe uttered a
sigh of relief when those words were spoken. But we are no
statesmen, and our task is not immediately practical but theoretical, although certainly not detached from the practical
interest. Therefore something is expected from us which cannot
be expected from a statesman. And it may be that there are
statesmen who are intensely interested in our doing our job,
which is not theirs.

Therefore I propose in these lectures to follow a path which
may appear a very bold one, and the difficulties of which are so
well known to us, that for a long while I hesitated to enter upon
it, but which seems to be a little more adequate to the depth of
the problem than most of the other more familiar ones. Let
me try to sketch it in a few words.

If by culture or civilisation—for the present not distinguishing
these concepts—we understand the sum of productions and
productive forces by which human life transcends the animal
or vital sphere of self-preservation and preservation of the
species, and if we ask by what factors such culture or civilisation
is determined, it seems that these factors can be subsumed under
three heads, in such a way that nothing essential is left out.
Civilisation is determined, first, by natural factors like formation
of country, climate, possibilities of maintenance, within which,
as a given frame, human life has to develop. Civilisation is
determined, secondly, by the physical and spiritual equipment
of men within a given area, by their physical and spiritual forces,
their vitality, their energy and their talent. These two com-
plexes we can put together as that which is outwardly and
inwardly *given*. Apart from these given factors, which are
inaccessible to human determination and freedom, there is a

third, which is just as important for the formation of a certain
civilisation in its specific character, namely the spiritual presuppositions of a religious and ethical nature which, not in
themselves cultural, we might call the culture-transcendent presuppositions of every culture.   This third factor lies within the
sphere of historical freedom, within that area which is open to
the free self-decision of man.   Assuming equal natural data and
equal physical and spiritual forces, two cultures will develop
differently if this third factor, the culture-transcendent presuppositions, is different.   It is this third factor which affords
the possibility for a spiritual force like Christianity to enter the
field of culture and give it a certain direction and character.
Once more assuming the natural data and the physical and
spiritual forces of two nations to be equal, the culture and civilisation within them will greatly differ, if the one is dominated by
the Christian religion and the other has another religion or an
irreligious conception of life, forming its culture-transcendent
factor.   This third factor then is the one within which the
Christian faith, as distinguished from its alternatives, becomes
relevant.

Now, within this third range, there are a number of fundamental basic questions regarding human existence which, in any
case, must be answered and are answered, whether in a Christian
or in a non-Christian manner.   Such questions are the problem
of being, of truth, of meaning, and so on.   Whether one is conscious of them or not, these questions are present; they must be
answered and the answer cannot be put off.   These culture-
transcendent presuppositions are working factors, and in their
totality they are one of the decisive elements within any given
civilisation.

It is just as false to consider these spiritual elements as the
one decisive factor—as has often been done by Christian theologians or idealistic philosophers,[8] as it is erroneous not to consider
them at all or to underrate their importance—as has often been
done by naturalist or positivist philosophers.   On one hand, it
must be affirmed that civilisation may be different in two given
areas, even if both are determined by the same spiritual factor,

e.g. by Christianity, presupposing that the natural conditions, and the physical forces and spiritual talents are different. On the other hand, it must be said that civilisation may be different in two given areas, although the natural conditions, physical forces and spiritual talents are the same. That means that each of the three groups of factors is decisive for the face and content of a civilisation. By civilisation we do not merely understand the narrower range of art, science and spiritual culture, but also economical and political forms and institutions. We, therefore, reject from the very start both a one-sided, spiritualising interpretation, which takes account merely of the third factor, the culture-transcendent presuppositions, and a one-sided naturalistic interpretation, which takes account only of the determining factors which are given in nature and man's natural equipment. The justification for this *a priori* starting point can be given only in the course of these lectures.

One thing, however, must be said at the start to justify our procedure. This procedure is a bold venture, because it ignores all traditional classifications of scientific investigation. To seek out those fundamental questions, underlying all human existence, seems to be a task for philosophy. At any rate, up to now, it has been the philosophers who have dealt with them. On the other side, we are not primarily concerned with philosophical answers to these questions, but with the answers which the Christian faith gives. And this seems to be a task for the theologians. At the same time, our investigation will not take place, so to say, in the empty space of thought, but within the concrete world of history and present-day life. For we are not merely interested in general abstract possibilities of a Christian civilisation, but in the possibility and the specific character of a Christian civilisation within this given historical world. And though our procedure is theoretical, our aim is intensely practical. Therefore I should not be surprised if what I am trying to do here were to be judged unfavourably by theologians as being philosophy, by philosophers as being theology, combined with a dilettante attempt at what in German is called *Geistesgeschichte* and *Gesellschaftskritik*. My reply to this

expected criticism is that I am just as much, but no more, convinced of the shortcomings of this attempt as of its necessity and
imperative urgency.

The point of view from which this investigation will be made
is that of Christian faith. Again, by Christian faith we do not
mean something indefinite, but the Gospel of the New Testament, as it is understood within the tradition of Reformation
theology. When therefore we ask, what is the Christian answer
to those elementary fundamental questions of human existence,
and what is the characteristic impact which this Christian
answer must have for the formation of civilisation, we mean by
Christian faith what, according to this specific tradition, the New
Testament means. But I want to make it clear from the very
start—impossible though it is to justify such a statement here—
that this position includes a critical attitude with regard to any
fixed dogma and an openness of mind and heart with regard
to all Christian tradition and knowledge. Reformation theology, truly understood, is neither uncritical orthodox Biblicism
nor self-assured exclusive confessionalism. It includes, on the
contrary, both the critical and the ecumenical attitudes. I am
sorry that the limitations imposed on these lectures do not allow
me to expound and prove these assertions, which are the result
of an extended process of critical theological self-examination.

Let me conclude what has been said by giving a final formulation of our problem. The problem of this first series of lectures
is to be stated in three questions:—

1. What answers does the Christian faith give to certain
fundamental questions of human existence which underlie any
civilisation as their culture-transcendent presuppositions?

2. How do these answers compare with other answers to
the same questions, as they occur in the course of Occidental
history?

3. What is the specific importance of the Christian answers
compared with that of the others? The following are the
questions which we have in mind or at least some of the most
important of them:—

The problem of being.
. The problem of truth.
The problem of time.
The problem of meaning.
Man in the universe.
Personality and humanity.
The problem of justice.
The problem of freedom.
The problem of creativity.

In trying to answer these questions we venture to outline in this first part a Christian doctrine of the foundations of civilisation, whilst the second part will deal with the more concrete problems of the different areas of civilised life.

II

THE PROBLEM OF BEING OR REALITY

WHAT is ? What is real ? What is appearance ? Perhaps it may seem strange that we start with this question, which is certainly not the one modern man asks. His question is: what is the meaning of life? Has life a meaning at all? The problem of being is foreign to him. It always has been foreign to non-philosophers; it seems to be a problem which exists only for the thinker. So it is, as a *conscious* problem. The ordinary man does not ask this question; for him it seems to be settled, he lives as if it were settled. He is not aware of the fact that his whole life is determined by an axiomatic conception of what is real.

That becomes clear if we ask what then is reality, God or the world, mind or matter, the visible or the invisible, the temporal or the eternal, the Many or the One? For the man of our time at any rate, whatever else he may consider as real, it is beyond question that sensible, tangible material things have the priority as regards certainty and weight of being. A realist is a man who tests reality by this criterion: material, sensible fact. The prevalent standard is still the primitive standard of physical condition. The most real thing is the hard, solid material, then follows the liquid, then the vaporous airy, transparent. The spiritual, therefore, is a further diminution of substantial reality, that which is farthest away from that most impressive reality of all, the heavy, impenetrable block of iron or stone. It is from this conception of reality that Ernst Haeckel defined God in conscious blasphemy as a gaseous vertebrate. On the other hand, if a Hindu calls Europeans materialists, he has in mind somehow this scale of realities which most Europeans take so much as a matter of course, that they cannot even understand that anyone might disagree and think differently about reality. This conception of reality, however, is by no means self-evident. Those who have been brought up within the Hindu tradition not only think, but feel, differently. It is not merely their theory, but implicit in their whole sense of life, that this material world is a phantom, an illusion which hides and falsifies our perceptions.

This is the feeling not only of those learned Brahmins who have studied the philosophy of the Upanishads. In the course of hundreds or even thousands of years something of this advaita-doctrine has become a common possession and has deeply influenced the sense of reality within the Indian world. Reality is not the many things which we can grasp and touch; reality is the One which we can never perceive with our senses. The more sensual, the more material, the less real. The true being is that which is farthest away from the material, and therefore is pure spirit; nay, even this assertion is still determined by that illusory world of the Many, and therefore not adequate. The true being is that which is beyond the opposition of mind and matter, subject and object, and therefore beyond definition by concepts, because definition as such is a limitation. Truly real is that indivisible One which, because indivisible, is also indefinable—Brahma.

This idea, which is so foreign to us and sounds so incredible, has held its own not only in India but also at certain times in Europe, in the form of Neoplatonic philosophy and mysticism, particularly within the so-called Christian mediæval world. The one true being, the ὄντως ὄν, as Plato called it, is the divine One, the ἕν καὶ πᾶν. True reality therefore is the spiritual, not the material world. A realist at that time was someone who affirmed the primary reality of the ideas of the spiritual world. Matter within that conception is, so to say, mind in a state of distension, obscuration, dismemberment, diffusion into what we in our time call substance. The mediæval thinker would have denied that attribute or qualification; substance to him was that which is unchangeable, that which has eternal duration, that which cannot be divided, the One and All.

Modern physics, paradoxical as it may seem at first sight, can bring us closer to an understanding of what mediæval man thought. In modern physics, reality is not substance, but energy, not something dead, fixed, stiff, but living power, tense, dynamic. No longer is energy an appearance of matter, it is matter that is an appearance of energy. Therefore it seems as if at the most unexpected point, in the science of matter, a revolution in the concept of being is in the making, a revolution in the direction of what we call mediæval Platonism or idealism. Leibnitz seems to be right: reality is to be found ultimately not in masses of matter, but in spiritual forces.

But perhaps this " either/or " is false, perhaps both extended matter and non-extended spirit are equally real, without being as such the ultimate reality. Since the Greek mind formed the concept of Cosmos, a mediating view of reality has been in existence. This world, which we see with our eyes and grasp with our hands, is somehow real. But what we grasp and see is not reality itself, but one of its aspects. Consummate reality is a totality, a world permeated by Logos, a unity of God and world, of mind and matter, of eternity and temporality, of transparent spirit and opaque weight. What the Greek with his plastic artistic mind expressed in his Cosmos idea, is something to which corresponds in some undefined manner a feeling which is basic in many peoples and which we find living in the primitive mind. Nature is permeated by divine spiritual forces, nature is always both, divine and immaterial, sensual and material. Reality is, like ourselves, animated body and materialised soul, divine nature and materialised divinity. Nature-forces are divine forces and deities are nature-forces. The one changes into the other, nay, the one is the other. This is also a feeling of many in our own day, expressing itself in the art and poetry of recent times in a most elementary way: reality is deeper than materialists think, our senses grasp only its surface, not its depth. Or better, surface and depth are one, the visible *is* the invisible and the invisible *is* the visible. Just this mystical unity is reality. " Natur hat weder Kern noch Schale, beides ist sie mit einem Male " (Goethe). This nature, identical with God, is reality.

The Christian understanding of reality is of a very different kind, totally unlike all these conceptions.[9] It is determined by the thought that God is the creator and the world His creation. God therefore is the primary reality. Whatever else we call real is secondary, dependent reality. This opposition of the divine and the creaturely beings seems at first hand very akin to that Neoplatonic distinction between the One, the real being and the Many which are not truly real. It would indeed be hard to understand how during so many centuries Christian theology and the Christian Church could have believed in the congruence if not identity of these two concepts, if there were not at least some similarity between these two conceptions of being. It is possible, as scholastic theology shows, to interpret the Neoplatonic idea of being in such a way that it becomes reconcilable with the Christian idea, if we assume on the other hand that the Christian idea has already been in some way adapted to the Neoplatonic one.[10] The common element in both is negative: this material tangible sense world is not, as the superficial mind believes, the true reality. Popular materialism or sensationalism is not reconcilable either with the Neoplatonic or with the Christian idea. The primary reality, the aboriginal being is God, and God is spirit.

This assertion, that God Who is spirit is the creator of all, has the most momentous consequences for the understanding of all existence.[11] All co-ordinates of the picture of reality—the above and the below, the whole system of weights, the whole hierarchy of values—and therefore the whole conception of culture and civilisation is determined by it. If God, the creator, *is*, then that gloomy idea of fate and fatality, which lies like a spell over the ancient as well as the modern world, loses its basis. It is not a fate, an impersonal, abstract determining power, not a law, not a something which is above everything that is and happens, but He, the creator spirit, the creator person.

If we take this idea seriously, we see at once an unbridgeable contrast between the Christian and the Neoplatonic idea of being. The Neoplatonic—and we may say also the idealistic and mystical conception of being—is impersonal; the Christian idea is personal. The Neoplatonic is static; the Christian is

active and dynamic.   God's being is the being of the Lord who
posits everything and is not posited.   Scholastic theology
rightly uses the concept of God as *actus purus*, unconditional
activity or actuality or actuosity.   God is therefore never
object, but always subject; never something—it, substance—but
He, or rather Thou.   God is absolutely free will, free in such a
way that the world, His creation, is at every moment conditioned
by His will.   Its being is like that of a soap bubble which exists
only because and as long as it is blown by the blower.   The
moment he ceases to blow it, it collapses into nothingness.   Of
course this simile falls short; the blower blows the bubble out
of a given liquid, God " blows " the world out of nothing, and
He holds it by His will through His *creatio continua* above the
abyss of nothingness.

    With this a second aspect of this idea of being is given, that
of creaturely, dependent being.   It is here that the contrast of
the Christian with the idealistic as well as the materialistic concepts becomes particularly clear.   For the materialist, *i.e.* one to
whom material, sensual being is the truly real, matter is a reality
of unquestionable, absolute solidity.   True, even he cannot but
see that all things are changing and passing.   But what changes,
he thinks, is not matter itself but merely the forms of matter.
The bearers of this unquestionable, absolute reality are the
elements, the chemical elements, the atoms.   The atomic theory
of Democritus was invented in order to maintain the conception
of absolute matter in face of the obvious change in the material
world.   It therefore was a profound shock to this—popular or
philosophical—materialism, when the latest results of physical
science pointed to the fact that there are no such unchangeable
material elements, that under the hands of the physicists this
substance was transformed into mere energy and mathematical
relations.   However that may be, according to Christian thought
there is no such imperishable, self-contained substance, but only
creaturely being, which exists because, and so long as, and such
as God wills it to be; being which He calls out of nothing and
which He holds above nothing.   It is, however, not only the
doctrine of creation, but equally Christian eschatology, with its

idea that this world at one time will be no more, which is deter-
minative for the Christian conception of creaturely dependent
being as distinguished from the being of God Himself.

This Christian idea of creaturely being is as radically different
from the idealist as from the materialist conception. This
created world is no mere appearance as idealism asserts. It is
reality. God has called it to be real. Its being is not stamped
with the mark of nothingness or degeneracy. What God has
created, that *is*, even if it is not independent but dependent
being. It is God Himself who gives it the weight of reality and
even of goodness. "And God saw every thing that He had
made and behold it was very good." The Neoplatonic idea
that everything which is not God is somehow degraded, degenerate, defective being, and the old idea of Plato that matter
as such is evil, is here impossible. Its being material does not
mean that a negative value is to be attached to material being;
in its place and within its limits it is good.

There is in Biblical thought as well as in that of Aristotle or
Plotinus a conception of a hierarchy of being, represented, for
instance, in the Genesis narrative of creation. The different
levels of the material, the organic, the animal and the human are
distinguished. But the lower levels are not thought of as less
real, nor as inferior. Everything which God has created, a
so-called lower being as well as a so-called higher one, has its full
positive value in its place. The idea—so fundamental in mediæval thought—that the hierarchy of being is also a hierarchy of
value, has no place within the Christian concept of the created
world. We shall see later what decisive importance this different valuation of the hierarchical structure of the world has for
the whole problem of ethics.

The Biblical idea of God the creator and the world as His
creation, in contrast to the Aristotelian and the Neoplatonic
conception of being, does not permit the idea of a continuum
in which God is the highest and matter the lowest point. God
is never to be seen in continuity with the hierarchy of the created
world. The distinction between God and creature is absolute;
the distinctions between the creatures, however, are relative.

There is no transition between created and the non-created being, God alone has non-created divine reality, and all creation has merely dependent, created reality. Between these two there are no intermediates. With this conception of creator and creation, the whole Cosmos idea and the corresponding pantheistic interpretation of nature, as we find it both in antiquity and in modern times, is exploded. The synthesis of the divine and of nature, of the infinite and finite is dissolved, and with it the foundation of paganism, which consists precisely in the affirmation of a transition between the divine and the world. All those conceptions of continuity between the finite and the infinite, the transcendent and this world, the divine and the earthly existence, that whole hierarchy of mythical figures, that scale reaching from the half divine hero to the highest of gods, or that interpenetration of nature and divinity which characterises the world concept of the primitive mind, as well as those sublime ideas of the world-permeating Logos making of the world a Cosmos, and every form of modern pantheism—all these are consumed by the fire of the idea of creation. No continuity whatever is left but the sharp opposition: Godhead on the one hand, the world's creatureliness on the other.

Of course this transcendence of God's *being* should never be confused with a transcendence of God's *activity*. The transcendent God—that is, the God who has the monopoly of divinity—is not separated from His creation. Distinction is not separation. God's being is distinguished from that of the world, but the world exists by His sustaining presence and activity. That God whom Goethe scorns (" Was wär' ein Gott, der nur von aussen stiesse "), is not the God of Biblical revelation, but of rationalistic deism. The God of revelation is the absolutely unworldly, the self-sufficient Lord, but He is the One who not only creates the world but sustains and rules it. He is the One by Whose will and action it is real and remains in existence, and without Whose presence and sustaining activity it would fall into nothingness. Every grain of sand depends on Him; without Him it passes into nothing.

Therefore it is only from the Christian idea of creation that

that which, in the philosophy of the Middle Ages, is called the contingency of being can be understood.[12] The distinction between the divine and absolute, and the contingent and relative being of created things is unknown to all the Greek philosophers. They either oppose the One, as the truly real, to mere appearance, or they think in terms of continuity, be it an upward continuum, like Aristotle, or a downward continuum, like Plotinus.

On the other hand, in the same degree that modern philosophy departs from the Christian idea of God, the distance between the contingent and the non-contingent disappears. For materialistic thinkers there is no contingent being. For them matter is the primary and absolute being. The atoms are unconditionally, absolutely real. Materialism attributes to the atoms the qualities which in Christian theology are attributes of God. According to materialistic thought they have the *a se esse*, they are eternal and independent beings. For the idealist only spirit or mind is real. The world, however, is mere appearance. There is no room for contingence in either case. This becomes of special importance in the interpretation of natural law as physics understands the term.

For the materialist, *i.e.* for the person whose conception of being is determined by matter, the laws of nature are absolute, objective entities inherent in material being. They are " die ewigen, unwandelbaren Gesetze " by which all being, all happening is determined. Again these natural laws play the rôle which in Christian thought is given to the will of God. They are the opposite of the contingent—the necessary. This is the blind, impersonal necessity of fate, which determines. everything. According to Laplace, a mind which at a given moment knew the site and motion of all atoms in the Universe would be capable of reconstructing all the past and to predict all the future, according to the laws of mechanics.[13] Everything is finished before it starts, nothing new can happen. But whilst we can easily understand that this determinism and fatalism is the natural and necessary consequence of a materialistic conception, it is rather surprising to observe that this idea of fate

lurks behind all pre-Christian religion and philosophy as well.
Fate is above all the Gods of mythology; Moira is above Zeus
and his Pantheon.   The sentences of the Norns decide the fate
of the highest Gods of Germanic religion.   The highest Gods
of Indian religion are powerless with regard to Karma, they
themselves are seized by the turning of the spinning wheel of
fate.   This coming and going is the expression of a higher,
unknowable, impersonal necessity.   And this is true also of all
Greek philosophy.   Neither Plato's " ideas " nor Aristotle's
"entelechy" nor the divine Nous of Stoicism or of Neoplatonism
breaks through this uncanny, gloomy determinism.   Why is
this so?   It is because all being which is conceived of in impersonal terms has the character of fate.   The personal Gods of
mythology are not absolute, and the Absolute of Greek philosophy is not personal.   There is but one alternative to fatalism
or determinism—the idea of God being almighty, sovereign
Lord, Whose freedom is above everything that is, and Whose
freedom is the cause of being of everything which is not Himself; the idea that God, the sovereign Lord, has created the world
out of nothing and can drop it into nothingness if He so wills.
He is that God, however, Whose will is not an unfathomable
secret, but revealed Love.   Whether there is a fate above everything or not is the same question as whether there is an
impersonal being or a personal absolute will above everything.
It seems to make little difference, however, whether this impersonal being be material or spiritual or an unknowable unity of
both.   Either fate or God the Creator!   From the Christian point
of view, then, natural laws are not absolute entities, but belong
themselves to the sphere of contingent relative being.   Natural
laws themselves are created.   They are, as we have it in the
German language, Ge-setze, i.e. " settings ".   God set them to be.
Now this conception of setting is ambiguous or ambivalent.
And this ambiguity of divine setting—Satzung, Gesetze—is a
fundamental trait of all Christian doctrine.   On the one hand,
God's settings, orders, laws, Gesetze are thought of as perma-
nent, static structures, as stable and dependable traits of the
God-created Universe.   You can rely upon these orders being

maintained; you can count on them; there is no disorder and arbitrariness in this world; it is an orderly world. But on the other hand these settings, laws and orders, being *given* by God, wants them to be. They are limitations for *our* freedom, not for His. His freedom is above all settings or laws, they are not fetters upon His action, and some day they shall be no more. For " the frame of this world perishes ". The contingent is also the transient, the perishable, the non-eternal.

Natural laws are not absolutes; behind and above them there is divine freedom. Natural laws are not ultimates, they are instrumental to God's purpose. They do not determine the purposes of God. They are organs, servants of His will. God's purposes can never be understood in terms of law. The law in every sense of the word has a subordinate, although a very important and indispensable function in God's economy. It has always to be reckoned with as a means of God, but it is never to be taken as an ultimate expression of God's will and purpose. It is therefore questionable whether we are justified in speaking of " eternal laws ". All laws, whether natural or moral, belong to the created world. God's own will can never be expressed ultimately in terms of law, because the freedom of His love as well as of His holiness is above them. If theology speaks of the law of God's own being, we must take care that we are not caught in our own words, putting abstractions above God's free will.

The physics of to-day, in distinction from that of Laplace's time, has made it possible again to hold fast the Biblical idea of God without getting into a conflict with natural law. Without entering the difficult and controversial consequences of the Quantum theory and without making a premature use of its startling results, we may safely say that the 18th and 19th century idea of an absolute world-determination by natural law, presupposing the idea of a " closed Universe " as pronounced by Laplace, has broken down. The idea of natural law will play its important and beneficent rôle in the future as it has done in the past. But it has ceased to play the rôle of an absolute world-dominant. There is room again for the acknowledgment of freedom, both divine and human.[14] But it is not physics, not even post-Planck-Einstein physics, that can break the spell of fatalism. That is done alone by the faith in God, the creator and Lord, as He is known through Biblical revelation exclusively.

I should like to draw from the Biblical idea of God a last consequence of ontology, which I shall call the "perspectivity" of being. Starting once more from the materialistic understanding of being, we find there as the guiding pattern the idea of the atom, the ultimate, material, unchangeable unit behind the changing, material happening. This atom *is*, whatever its definition in terms of physics may be, whether it is the Elektron or Proton or Neutron or what may be; it is, irrespective of where it is, from where you see it, or who sees it. It is, to use Kant's word, a " Sein an sich ", or " ein an sich Seiendes ". This objectivism, which philosophy for many a day has called naive realism, was exposed as an impossibility many centuries ago. There is no such "an sich Seiendes", because being is always correlative to a subject for which it is being. This critical idealism has an easier task to-day than at the time of Berkeley or Kant. At that time there was still in existence the insuperable contrast between the so-called primary and secondary qualities of things. It is quite obvious that there is something sweet only for a tongue which tastes it and a mind which passes the judgment that it is sweet. But that a pound is a pound and a metre a metre, independent of a subject, seemed to be just as clear. Now, since Einstein, there are no "metres in themselves" left. What is a metre within one system of reference may not be a metre within another, and that means also that the so-called primary qualities have become relative to an observing subject. "Perspectivism" has broken the spell of naive objectivism in the very field of physics. With that knowledge, an old philosophical thesis of idealism has been confirmed. Plato finally has overcome Democritus.

None the less, this idealistic conception of being has never been capable of convincing definitely. However compelling its arguments, there was an aboriginal realistic instinct which did not give way to this contention. That there is nothing independent of himself as knowing subject is what no one will believe. To the ordinary man philosophical idealism always appeared as a sort of semi-lunacy, at least an eccentricity. The philosopher by his superior power of thinking could feel himself superior to the average man and to the judgment of common sense. But what remained a worrying fact, even for him, was that in his practical life he was a naive realist, just as much as his philosophical opponents. There is another observation which cannot be omitted at this point: it seemed to be impossible, at least very difficult, not to step over the limit which separates critical and speculative idealism and thus develop a system akin to that of Neoplatonic metaphysics with its idea of ἓν καὶ πᾶν, the One and All, i.e. absolute spiritualism which denies a reality apart from or besides that One and All.

To return to the starting point of our lecture, the Christian conception of God the Creator, and of the world as His creation, is neither that of naive realism nor that of speculative idealism; in structure as in origin it is different from both. God, Who is spirit, is the primary original being and the world is dependent secondary being. That is to say that the world *has* objective reality, not in itself, but through the thought and will of the Creator. It *is*, but it is what God thought and willed it to be before it was. Everything which objectively is, is (1) an idea of God, (2) a realisation of His will, and therefore has reality only *because* it is God's idea and will. Where does our knowledge of this being come from? The answer to this question, I think, is this: we can *know* it exactly because it is an idea. If it were not an idea, knowledge could not penetrate it, it would be simply irrational. Now, being objective, world-being to us is both knowable and unknowable, rational and irrational. Our mind finds something to know. The light of our mind is capable of clearing up something of the objective reality, but it cannot make it transparent. There always remains something opaque, dark, resisting the perspicacity of knowledge. This *is* so because created being is not *merely* an idea of God, but is at the same time a setting of His *will*, and therefore irrational for our knowledge. It is factuality, that element of givenness, which is always

the limit of our knowledge and at the same time exactly that
element which produces in us the feeling of reality, transcending
our knowledge.

From the Christian point of view, then, idealism is right in
saying that there is no object without a subject which posits this
being. But it is wrong in thinking that it is *our* subject which
posits this reality. It is not our, but God's subject, which posits
reality. It is ours only in so far as our thinking gets a share in
God's own thought, as the psalmist says: "In Thy light shall we
see light".[15] On the other hand, our knowledge, however it
may extend or be extended, always comes to grief at a certain
limit, and it is precisely this limit which is the test of reality.
It is just because our knowledge comes to grief at this dark,
opaque something which it cannot penetrate, that we say "this
is real". But we are not capable of uniting both the light of
knowledge and the darkness of irrational givenness, except in
the one thought, that God is the creator, by Whose thought it
is "rationable", by Whose will it is irrationally "given".[16]

I cannot but heartily agree therefore with Karl Barth, when
in his doctrine of creation he formulates that sentence, which at
first sight seems absurd, that the reality of the objective world
becomes certain to us only in the faith or belief in God the
Creator,[17] that is to say, in that faith in that Creator who reveals
Himself in His own word.

It is only by drawing this consequence of a divine "perspectivism" that what we said about contingence becomes convincing. The world around us is God's creation, that is why it is at
once objectively real and subjectively ideal. It has not absolute
reality, but in the strictest sense of the word relative, conditioned
reality through God's positing it. It therefore takes part in the
ambiguity or ambivalence which we have just been observing
as the character of natural laws; it is real because, and in so far
as, God realises it. It ceases to be real as soon as God ceases to
realise it. It is possible that this insight may be the key to
certain problems of Christian theology, *e.g.* of eschatology,
which seem to us insoluble and which burden our theological
conscience. But there is no room here to develop these

consequences lying, as they do, beyond the horizon which we have drawn for these lectures.

If we deal with these problems of ontology, the first impression will always be that they are of a very abstract nature and far from the ordinary problems of life. I do hope, however, that I may have imparted to you some feeling that these are questions of most practical importance, even for the ordinary man in the street. The whole feeling of life, the whole orientation of existence must be very different according to whether one is the kind of man to whom material atoms are the measure of all reality, or the kind to whom all this is a mere illusion, or the kind who thinks in terms of his faith in the Creator and speaks to us in the 139th Psalm:

> O Lord, thou hast searched me, and known me.
> Thou knowest my downsitting and mine uprising.
> Thou understandest my thought afar off.
> Thou searchest out my path and my lying down,
> And art acquainted with all my ways
> For there is not a word in my tongue
> But, lo, O Lord, thou knowest it altogether.
> Thou hast beset me behind and before,
> And laid thine hand upon me.
> Such knowledge is too wonderful for me ;
> It is high, I cannot attain unto it.
> Whither shall I go from thy spirit ?
> Or whither shall I flee from thy presence ?
> If I ascend up into heaven, thou art there :
> If I make my bed in Sheol, behold, thou art there.
> If I take the wings of the morning,
> And dwell in the uttermost parts of the sea ;
> Even there shall thy hand lead me,
> And thy right hand shall hold me.

I had to quote this Psalm literally and at some length because it is such a perfect summary of what I have been trying to say. The world around us is real; but God Himself is much more real, and therefore much more present. The things of the world we have at a distance; but He is as near to us as our eye, as our thinking mind. That God sees us, that He sees me and looks upon me, this is the central, all-determining assertion of the

Biblical message. Let me put it, that this is the " perspectivism " of divine election. How fundamental this idea is for all our cultural problems we shall see as soon as we have grasped the necessary connections of this idea with that of human personality. Before we can enter on this problem, however, we shall have to deal with some others of a more abstract nature, the first of them being the question of truth.

III

THE PROBLEM OF TRUTH

THE problem of truth is so intimately and inseparably connected with that of being that neither cannot be dealt with apart from the other. Therefore the old question as to which of the two has the priority can hardly be definitely settled.

It cannot be doubted, however, that for primitive man, as well as for the average man of our times, the question of truth is no other than that of reality. Truth and reality are one for him. As a matter of fact, the question "What is truth?" is first asked only at the moment when what has hitherto been believed to be real becomes more or less doubtful. The question of truth stands on the borderline between naive dogmatism and nascent scepticism. It is the critical question.

The spiritual state of our time is characterised by curious paradoxes. On one hand, modern man is a naive realist—even a dogmatist or absolutist—the material, sensual data being to him unquestionable reality. If he speaks of reality in terms of indisputable certainty, he points to the material world, to the world of space, filled with matter. But it so happens that modern science has shattered and riddled this compact conception of the world in such a way that modern man, without giving up his naive conception of reality, has at the same time become a sceptic. It is not the first time in the history of thought that scepticism and materialism have gone hand in hand.[18] Those things which are the measure of all truth for the naive dogmatist somehow betray man by withdrawing themselves suddenly from him, leaving him alone with the open question whether they exist at all. So it is not very surprising that those who at one time hold a thoroughly materialistic view of reality should, at another time, adopt an unqualified relativism or scepticism.

The phrase " Everything is relative " is spoken emphatically by the very people for whom the atom or its elements are still the ultimate reality. Everything is relative, they say, but at the same time they declare as indubitable truth that the mind is nothing but a product of cerebral processes. This combination of gross objectivism and bottomless subjectivism represents a synthesis of logically irreconcilable, contradictory principles of thought, which is equally unfortunate from the point of view of philosophical consistency and from that of ethical and cultural value.

Apart from this last sceptical stage, it must be said that modern spiritual evolution has been taking unambiguously the line of a more or less materialistic objectivism. This chapter of human history could be headed—to parody Kierkegaard's phrase—" The object is the truth! " It cannot, then, be a surprise to see man more and more engulfed in the object, in things, in material being, in economic life, in technics, in a one-sided, quantitative manner of thinking, and in quantitative standards of value. In the sphere of material being the quantum is the only differentiating factor. Material being is merely quantitative being. An objectivist understanding of truth expresses itself, therefore, not merely in terms of practical materialism, but also in a general quantification of all life, as it may be seen in the craving for records in sport, in pride in the growth of cities of millions of inhabitants, in respect for the multi-millionaire, in admiration for great political power. Reverence for the quantum is, so to speak, the new version of the worship of the golden calf. It is an inevitable consequence of the objectivist conception of truth: The object is the truth.

That the development of the Western mind should have followed this unfortunate line is by no means inevitable; indeed one might even ask whether Immanuel Kant and his predecessors and successors, whose philosophy had pointed in the opposite direction, have lived in vain? Was it not the main tenet of idealistic philosophy that the subject, not the object, is the truth; that the mind, not the thing, is the true reality? Since Plato worked out this revolutionary conception of truth, idealism has been one of the great powers in the life of Western mankind. The question here did not concern merely the theoretical philosophy of knowledge, but in a vital degree, man and mankind in its totality. Once the spell of objectivism is broken, once man has become aware of a reality different from that of things, the road is open for a supremely rich development of spiritual life in all directions. Those who know something of the enormous contribution of idealism to European life cannot but pay it a high tribute and recall its great exponents with deep reverence. Who can help being impressed by the greatness and sublimity of idealistic thought, as manifest in Herder's *Ideen zur Philosophie der Geschichte der Menschheit*, in Humboldt's essay on the limits of the state? Who can resist Schiller's passion for free humanity, springing from this fountain? Who would not be uplifted and feel his spiritual horizon widened on entering the thought-world of Hegel's philosophy of history?

And yet all this beautiful world is as if perished; all the idealistic spirituality of the last two centuries appears now like the flash of a meteor in the night sky. Such idealism has ceased to be a spiritual power among mankind and, looking back, we cannot help questioning whether it ever was a spiritual power, in its own strength. It was a power, of that there is no doubt. But was it not so only as long as it was combined with the Christian tradition, an undertone—or, if you prefer, an overtone—of the Christian message which ceased to sound when the main note disappeared?

We have to ask why that was so: why this idealism, which at the end of the 18th and the beginning of the 19th century broke forth so powerfully and seemed invincible, broke down so rapidly and was completely carried away by the waves of naturalism and materialism? Two observations impose themselves of which, however, only the first seems to be directly connected with our topic—the idea of truth—whilst the second seems to belong to an entirely different range of problems. The first observation is this: that this reversal from the object to the subject was an idea which could never become a universal

conviction in our Western world as it had become in India.
This idealistic subjectivism remained a queer, philosophical
tenet, a speciality of a tiny elite of chosen thinkers. It would
be a most instructive and fascinating study to trace in the early
writings of Karl Marx (dating from the time when he was an
enthusiastic pupil of Hegel), the complete right about turn which
led him from the absolute idealism of Hegel to a gross materialism, a process which we cannot fail to observe, not only in the
development of Marx, but also in that of two other pupils of
Hegel, Anselm Feuerbach and David Friedrich Strauss. This
all-embracing spirituality, so to say, toppled over; this excess
evaporated like a kind of spiritual intoxication, and what
remained was the depression of a barren materialism. The
way that Marx and Feuerbach went is very instructive. The
tenet, " The subject, Mind (*Geist*), is the truth ", changed into a
positivist anthropologism; the transcendental Ego changed into
the psychological fact of empirical consciousness of that man,
who, taken as a whole, is part of this world of things. Feuerbach's famous thesis, " All theology is anthropology ",[19] meant
the complete desertion of the idealistic line. It was the
equivalent of looking upon everything metaphysical as a mere
phantasm. This is what Hegel's idealistic philosophy led to in
his most gifted pupils.

Among these, Marx is the only one who made history. His
name stands, not without good reason, for a whole world : the
world of the proletarian man, the socialist-communist worker's
movement, and a " Weltanschauung " based on the collectivist
conception of man. Idealism offered no solution for the problem
of society. It was a matter for the highly educated individual,
for an intellectual aristocracy. What the philosophical and
literary giants at Weimar or Jena, or around the newly created
University of Berlin, were discussing and writing did not touch
the millions of common people whom modern machinery had
thrown out of their rural, patriarchical conditions into giant
industrial cities, and there pounded together like coal-dust into
the briquets of collectivist masses. Idealism, with its theory
that mind, reason, spirit, subject is the truth, had no answer to

the question, "What is to happen to these people?" That is why it did not survive.

Objectivist materialism, on the other hand, remains in some way within the apparent reality of man. Man is an animal, with appetite, and therefore must be fed. Man is a gregarious animal, living in flocks with his kind, in order to face the common foe against which the individual would be too weak. Such is the view of man when the object is regarded as the truth. Man, in conceiving of himself as object, conceives of himself as an animal with the instinct for feeding and procreation and, therefore, as a gregarious animal. Objectivism necessarily leads to collectivism. If the object is the truth, man is merely an individual of a species, a part of nature. It may be added, however, that this view cannot be taken without the concomitant sceptical thought that probably there is no truth at all. In the collectivist society of Russia, for example, the search for truth is out of date.

We ask next whether there can be an understanding of truth beyond these two half-truths of objectivism and subjectivism and more credible than either. Can there be an understanding of truth which, at the same time, would be a solution of the problem of community? Within the last generation we have seen springing up more or less spontaneously in different areas, and moving on parallel lines, a series of attempts to tackle the problem of truth in a new fashion, namely in such a way that the old opposition of objectivism and subjectivism no longer plays the dominating rôle. Perhaps it is possible to view in this perspective the original form of pragmatism as set forth in the writings of William James. Certainly the phenomenology of Husserl and such philosophies as those of Max Scheler and Martin Heidegger (both being descendants of Husserl) and, above all, the discovery of the I-Thou relation connected with the names of Ebner, Buber and Grisebach, are attempts to get beyond the subject-object opposition.[20] All of the last-named thinkers have undergone the influence of Sören Kierkegaard. It was he who, more than anyone else, disclosed the unreality of Hegel's idealistic thoughts, pointing to the problem of existing man. But what Kierkegaard contributed to European thought was nothing but original Christianity and the Christian understanding of truth.

If God is the primary reality, then the word of God is the primary truth. Thus truth is not to be found either in the object or in the subject, but beyond both. Truth, then, is God Himself in His self-communication to man. If this is the truth, objectivism in its crudest form—materialism—is unmasked as idolatry, as deification of the world. But then subjectivism too, even in its most impressive form as absolute idealism, is idolatry as well, namely deification of the Ego, the absolute Ego of Ficl..e, which creates the non-Ego by itself; or the Atman-principle of Indian philosophy, which is identical with Brahma, the divine reality; or that Nous of Greek idealism which ultimately identifies the human Nous with the divine; or the absolute principle of Reason in its different forms, underlying the various systems of newer Occidental philosophy.

If it is true that the word of God is the truth, we have first to distinguish between Truth in the singular—which means God—and truths in the plural—which are truths about the world. As God is the Creator (and as such the primary reality) and the world His creation (and as such derived, conditioned and relative reality, having its ground in God), so there are also two kinds of truths: God-truth and world-truths. It is one of the great tragedies of Christian history that this distinction has not been carried through. Mediæval theology—and with regard to this question Protestant orthodoxy takes the same view—considered the source of God-truth, revelation, Holy Scripture, as being also the truth and norm of world-knowledge. By so doing it has fettered the legitimate, scientific use of reason and stamped the world-picture of Biblical antiquity with the authority of divine revelation. Thus Copernicus had to be called a fool, and his successor, Galileo, accused of heresy, because their teaching about the structure of the astronomical world was irreconcilable with the Biblical picture. For the same reason Darwin had to be called an enemy of God because he placed man as a " zoon " within the great connection of the animal world. The Church conducted a miserable crusade against the young, serious and high-spirited scientific generation seeking truth—world-truth—at all cost.

Retribution was bound to come. Science paid the Church back, so to speak, in the same coin: in its turn it failed to distinguish between God-truth and world-truths. More and more, science claimed the monopoly of truth-knowledge. The positivistic view that only scientific knowledge has a legitimate claim to truth, and that nothing which is incapable of scientific proof can be true—this orthodoxy of scientific positivism, forming an exact parallel with mediæval clerical orthodoxy—not merely has its following among philosophers and scientists, but has become a very popular and wide-spread creed. This is the tenet: *Science* is the truth. The road to truth is science. Whatever lies outside the range of science has no claim to truth. Nothing can be aknowledged as truth that does not carry the *placet* of science. Now, once this theoretical absolutisation of science is established, its practical deification cannot but follow. Science is held to be the salvation of the world, science will solve the practical problems of humanity, science will play the rôle which, in older times, was ascribed to God. Intoxicated by the astounding progress of physics, chemistry and biology, swept off his feet by his successful storming of the secret of atomic energy, modern man—particularly modern, scientifically trained youth —expects from the progress of science the solution of all problems of life.

This fantastic exaggeration of the possibilities of scientific knowledge and its technical applications is hardly intelligible to those who have become aware of the distinction between God-truth and world-truths, and therefore see the insurmountable limitation of scientific knowledge. But even among those who do not hold the Christian point of view, and therefore cannot make this distinction between God-knowledge and world-knowledge, there are many who recognise at least one limitation of scientific knowledge. They have come to see that science can never speak with authority about *ends,* but only about means, that it cannot find the *meaning* of anything, but only facts, and that science can therefore do nothing within that region in which human disorder has become most apparent—namely in the sphere of human relationships, the sphere of ethical, social and political problems. It has become clear—particularly through the technical application of scientific discoveries in the field of nuclear physics as, for instance, the atomic bomb—that we are facing a tragic discrepancy between the infinite means of power placed at our disposal by science and its beneficial use in human life. This fact has made many scientists and thinking people at large realise that even science stands under the primacy of ethical norms which in themselves are beyond scientific knowledge.

But man, when he is possessed by the idea of object-truth, thing-credulous man, who cannot but think in terms of quantity, whose eyes are blind to all that belongs to the sphere of quality, cannot comprehend this situation. Combined with materialism and with its derivative, collectivism, his faith in the saving power of science has created something like a technocratic religion, in which fanaticism and absolute soullessness, thing-credulity and absolute person-blindness has created a new kind of humanity, characterised by the most dreadful inhumanity, of which those who still know something of spiritual and personal culture cannot but think with horror.[21] This is the fruit of positivism, of the deification of science.

The distinction between world-knowledge and God-knowledge —leaving to scientific investigation the world of facts and reserving for divine revelation the disclosure of the mystery of God's being,[22] will and purpose—is not the only revolution which the Christian faith produces within the realm of the concept of truth. There is a second, just as important. What kind of a truth is it, then, which is revealed to faith? It is not truth in the sense of knowing something, but in the sense of a divine-human, personal encounter. God does not reveal this and that; He does not reveal a number of truths. He reveals Himself by communicating Himself. It is the secret of His person which He reveals, and the secret of His person is just this, that He is self-communicating will; that God is Love.

It is not possible to discuss fully here the depth and width of the Christian doctrine of God and His holy merciful will. I can only hint at the fact that the central Christian doctrine—the doctrine of the Trinity—has exactly this meaning, that the mystery of God's being is communion. Not merely does He reveal His will-to-communion with us, His creatures; He reveals Himself, His very essence as Love, as self-communicating Life. The mystery of the Trinity is the mystery of the Love-Life in God. This is a knowledge which stands beyond all analogies of philosophical theology or religious conceptions of God. It has no parallel whatever. That God is, in Himself, self-communicating Love—this is the doctrine of the Bible alone. Now, this is to say that truth is thereby identical with the good in its highest sense—love, communion. The fatal breach between theoretical and practical reason, between knowledge of truth and ethical will, is thus healed. The solution of the problem of ultimate truth—truth identical with ultimate absolute reality— is at the same time the solution of the ethical and social problem. The man who, by revelation and faith, takes part in the divine truth, at the same time takes part in the divine love, and is therefore taken into communion. To be in truth is to be in the Love of God, and to be in the Love of God is to become a loving person, to be in communion both with God and men.

If we look back we can see that to have fixed the problem of truth on the object-subject opposition is the disastrous error in Western spiritual history. Ultimate, final, absolute truth is neither the object nor the subject, neither the things nor the mind nor reason. The either/or of objectivism and subjectivism rather hides than reveals what is ultimately true. Whether the knowing subject or Ego posits itself as the truth, or whether it posits as truth its known object—" something ", in neither case is this relation one which discloses ultimate truth. God is neither our known object, nor is He our knowing subject; He is the self-communicating, absolute subject. Or, as the Biblical language expresses it, He is the Lord.

So long as truth is thought of within the subject-object dichotomy, it is unavoidable that either the subject or the object

becomes God, the ultimate truth and reality. Now, since neither
the subject nor the object is the ultimate truth, it is inevitable
that man's mind shifts from one pole to the other in an incessant
pendulum movement. It cannot rest quietly with either of the
alternatives, since neither of them carries real conviction. This
veering from objectivism into subjectivism and back is unavoidable, because in the long run neither of these two answers to the
question of truth is credible. How should the object, the world
of things, be the truth, when the subject, the knowing, thinking
Ego stands above it? How should the known be more than the
knower? On the other hand, how should the subject be the
ultimate truth whilst there is a world assigned to it, whatever it
may be, in impenetrable reality? Fichte may throw his philosophy of the absolute Ego into the world of the Enlightenment
as " sonnenklarer Bericht ",[23] but it will not be long before there
is an Ernst Haeckel in the field offering his gross materialism
as the solution of all the riddles of the Universe. And for
one reader whom Fichte may find there will certainly be a
hundred or even a thousand who will buy Haeckel's book as the
last word of pure scientific knowledge.

But if it is true, as faith knows it to be true, that God's word
is the truth, it means that truth—absolute, ultimate, final truth—
is not " something " that I can know as an object opposite me,
neither is it reason or spirit, my knowing mind, but it is the
divine Thou who, in His own initiative, discloses Himself to me.
True, God is over against me, yet He is no object, but spirit.
True, He is spirit, but not my spirit; He is the absolute subject,
which I am not. In disclosing Himself to me as the absolute
spirit or Ego, as my Lord, as one who says, " I am the Lord, thy
God!", He does not become the object of my knowledge. The
God of revelation is never my knowledge-possession. In making
Himself known to me, He makes me totally His own. If we
were to use here the categories " subject " and " object ", we
should have to say: In this truth-relation I am the object of this
subject. This is exactly what the Apostle means when he says:
To know God truly is to be known by God.[24] And this fact—
that God knows me and reveals Himself to me as the one who

knows me—is nothing else than what the Bible terms election, that election which is the sovereign act of His freely given divine Love.

This is what the Christian message calls finding the truth. Now we can understand why the Gospel says, "I am the truth!"[25] Ultimate truth, identical with ultimate reality, is not "something", but God in His revelation in His word. And this word of God is not merely a word about God, but that word in which He encounters me as person, and that person in which God encounters me as truth.[26] This is the incarnate word in which the eternal mystery of the divine personality discloses itself in a historical person. But, again, this disclosure or revelation of God's truth cannot take place in an "objective" act of knowledge, but in such a way that it discloses, at the same time, the solitary, egotistic human subject for the divine Love, and thereby transforms it.

Is it then historical truth? Yes and no. Yes, for it is in history that this revealed secret encounters me as truth. No, for it is the eternal God who now speaks to me in this historical revelation. Thereby the historical event ceases to be historical and becomes living presence. It is by present inspiration that past incarnation becomes truth to me. It is by this historical revelation of the incarnate word that this present inspiration can take place.

This truth, we said, is not truth which I possess, but truth which possesses me. In this context the Bible uses an expression which is unknown to philosophy, "To be in truth". This does not mean merely ethical truthfulness, though this ethical truthfulness is certainly included. But to be "in" truth means much more: it means the same thing as to be in Christ, the same as to be in God's Love. Where this truth is known, something happens within the centre of the knowing subject. To know this truth does not mean, as is the case with ordinary knowledge, to become richer, enlarged, enhanced. To know this truth means to be transformed. To be in this truth means to become a new creature, a new kind of being. Being-in-truth means being-in-love. It is not mere knowledge that is given here, but communion. To know this truth is to become a loving person.

Once more we look back on the history of the truth-problem. Its unfortunate development is marked not merely by the setting up of the object-subject-opposition, but also by the dissociation of truth and communion, of the true and the good. From Plato onwards we see the knowledge of truth developing in a direction which isolates individuals instead of gathering them into communion. Whether man seeks truth in the object—in things, or in the subject—in mind or spirit, in either case knowledge of truth does not create communion. Either it creates the isolated spiritual individual or it creates collectivism; science and technics do not really unite mankind. What modern technics do is to create combinations of a thoroughly impersonal character. On the other hand, idealistic philosophy had an effect similar to that of mysticism, though not to the same degree; it makes the individual independent not only of the world, but also of his fellow man, since it considers the development of the spiritual personality the ultimate purpose.[27] Idealism always leads to some kind of individualism; materialism, on the other hand, to some kind of collectivism. It is only in the Christian concept of truth that truth and communion are identical. Truth is love, because God is Love.

It would be utterly false, however, to pass this critical judgment upon our spiritual history from the viewpoint of a self-assured Christianity, of a pharisaical churchliness. We have already pointed out that empirical Christianity has sadly sinned against its own truth in not distinguishing between God-truth and world-truths, or at least in not distinguishing them consistently. But there is a second, even more serious failure to be mentioned: the identification of revealed God-truth and fixed dogma. In the very place where St. Paul says that knowing God means to be known by God, he uses the famous phrase which the dogmatising Church unfortunately never took seriously: " We know in part " (" Unser Wissen ist Stückwerk "). Even that which we know by God's revelation, we know only in part. It is absolute truth merely in so far as it is God's word;

formulated by us as our knowledge, it at once becomes part in the whole weakness and imperfection of our human condition. God's revelation identified with human dogma is the transformation of God-truth into world-truth. Now this is the general formula for metaphysics: metaphysics is the extension of the process of acquiring world-knowledge into the realm of God-knowledge, it is God-truth in the form of world-knowledge. Within metaphysics the absolute truth, God, is something knowable, a part of man's own realm of knowing. I think it is this which Kant had in mind when attacking all metaphysical theology. But we are not concerned here with the philosophical criticism of metaphysics; whatever metaphysics may be for the philosopher, from the Christian point of view it is a grave misunderstanding. Even more, it is a kind of idolatry, identifying God with the product of our own thought.

It is exactly this which underlies the dogmatism of the Christian Church, *i.e.* the false identification of God's revelation and our formulation of it which takes place as soon as one forgets the basic truth that "we know in part". The Church dogma, taken as absolute, springs from the innate tendency of man to absolutise his own knowledge of truth. Like all dogmatism, and more than any other, it has produced an obduracy of mind and heart. It has fettered necessary spiritual freedom and anathematised critical examination, thus evoking in reaction a hostile attitude towards the teaching of the Church, which has taken the form either of a rationalist dogmatism or of a relativist scepticism.

But there were even graver consequences. Church dogmatism has made almost impossible the truly Christian understanding of truth. For centuries, inside and outside the Church, it produced and sustained the false conception that faith or belief means to accept certain revealed truths taught by the Church or the Bible, which have to be accepted on their authority. This erroneous conception of faith as a heteronomous, authoritarian belief—as submission to the authority of the teaching Church or to that of the Bible—has become an almost insuperable hindrance to true faith-knowledge. Where this false conception of faith prevails—where faith or belief is understood as an acceptance of doctrines instead of a divine-human encounter— it is no longer the unity of truth and communion, and therefore no longer the faith which cannot but work itself out in love. This orthodox dogmatism has separated faith and love, and produced a kind of believer in whose life love is not the characteristic feature. For this reason the Church bears a large part of the responsibility for the misunderstanding of the truth-problem which so unfortunately characterises our history.

To sum up, the genuinely Christian understanding of truth is such that it allows all necessary freedom for scientific investigation of the world and at the same time guards against the misunderstanding that science holds the key to the mystery of human existence and is the source and norm for ultimate truth. The divine knowledge given to faith does not merely fulfil the highest endeavour after truth, but at the same time brings man into communion with God and man. Whilst in ancient philosophy the unity of truth and goodness was dimly felt or aspired after but not known,[28] and whilst in modern times the search for truth and the search for community have led in diverging directions, this unity of truth and communion comes through the revelation of God, Who is the ground of all reality and the source of all good. This genuine Christian understanding, however, sits in judgment not only upon modern spiritual development, leading consciously and unambiguously away from Christianity, but also upon empirical Christendom itself, which has hidden that true understanding by its dogmatism. The great promise of St. John's Gospel, that truth shall make us free, was not fulfilled by traditional Christianity, and still less by modern intellectualist conceptions of truth. Neither science nor the Christian dogma has proved to be the liberating power. Science stands bewildered and helpless before the ethical and social chaos of our time. And the dogmatism of the Christian Church has discredited the truth of revelation and hidden it from those who seek a real solution of this chaos. But wherever the genuine, original truth of revelation in its New Testament purity and depth is grasped by, or rather gets hold of, man, there forces of moral renewal and a spirit of communion are created, which alone are capable of reuniting that self-dissolving human family and of solving the problems of society. It is there, also, that the old problem of science and belief, faith and knowledge, is seen as a misunderstanding and ceases to exist, because it is possible to give to science what belongs to science, and to revelation what belongs to revelation, and still see their unity in the One who has created this world different from Himself, and has reserved to Himself the revelation of the mystery of His own being and will.

IV

THE PROBLEM OF TIME

THE relation of man to time is an essential factor determining the character of existence for the individual, as well as for whole epochs and different civilisations. Everyone knows that the haste and rush which characterise our life are something typically modern, and probably a symptom of a deep-seated disease. But there are few who take account of the basic elements which determine man's relation to time. It is not because modern man has watches and time-saving machinery that his life shows an ever-increasing speed; modern man has watches and time-saving machinery because he has a certain relation to time, which expresses itself most crudely in that often heard phrase: I don't have time! Now that even children in the nursery use this phrase, we can no longer postpone investigating the roots of the apparent time-disease of the present world.

All who have travelled in the East with open eyes and an impressionable mind are at one in finding an immense contrast between the quiet of the Orient and the unrest of the West. Although we cannot deny that certain external elements of technical civilisation contribute towards this striking difference, its real cause does not lie on this superficial level, but in a different relation to time. The Orient has a conception of time entirely different from that of the West, and this difference belongs to the religious and metaphysical sphere. In all Oriental philosophy and religion, time is something irrelevant and illusory compared with eternity, although the individual interpretations of this basic conception may differ. Reality is beyond and above the time-process. Change means imperfection. Just as a man looking for change does so because he is not satisfied with what he has, so nothing that is subject to change can be looked upon as true being. That which exists must have duration, persistence; it must be changeless, being satisfied with itself. It is not possessed by an urge to get what it does not have, to become what it is not yet. True being is eternal. This idea is common to the whole Eastern world, however differently this eternal being may be interpreted. The radical expression of this idea is again found in India. The world of change is unreal. Reality is—as we heard in a previous lecture—the One and All which cannot change, and therefore has no relation to time. It is timeless, motionless, self-satisfied eternity; therefore it is the deepest desire of the Indian thinker to enter into or to share in that motionless eternal being, in Nirvana.

This conception, however, was not foreign to ancient Greece. We find it in its most daring expression in the system of Parmenides, and in a less extreme form in Plato's idealism. The ὄντως ὄν, the true being of the world of ideas, is distinguished from mere appearance or the half-reality of the world of sensations by this very fact, that it is timeless eternity beyond all change. This world of sensible experience, however, is taken up with an incessant stream of change and becoming. There is a clear-cut opposition between eternity and the temporal world. Eternity is the negation of time: time is the negation of eternity. How this time-world came into being, and what kind of being it has, is a question which can hardly be answered satisfactorily from Plato's presuppositions. On the one hand, Plato wants to get away from the blunt negation of the temporal world as represented by Parmenides; on the other hand, he does not seem to succeed in giving the world of time and becoming its proper place. Neoplatonism which, as we have already seen, is so important for the formation of the mediæval world, tried to solve the problem by the concept of emanation, emanation meaning at the same time a kind of degeneration. By a process of flowing out or going down, a whole hierarchy of half-realities is established between the eternal, true being and absolute nothingness. In this hierarchy the distance of each step from the eternal is also its distance from true being or the measure of its approach to nothingness. Thus a continuum reaching from eternal true being to zero is conceived, which forms a parallel to the modern concept of evolution but runs in the opposite direction.

Modern man's understanding of time is quite different from this conception. To him the temporal is the real. Whether there is anything eternal is uncertain; but that the things in time are, is beyond question. But what is his concept of time? As it is quantity which determines his concept of reality, time also is a quantum—measurable time, time which consists of time-units, time-atoms. The second hand of the watch is the symbol of modern man's understanding of time. He looks for reality in the present moment, but the present moment is the smallest indivisible element or fraction of time. Life, then, cannot be but the sum or addition of such fractional time-entities, of time-atoms. This quantified physical time has completely lost its distinctiveness from space; it has become a fourth dimension of space.[29] Quantified time is spatialised time. Time dwindles away into space. It has no quality of its own. It is interchangeable with the dimensions of space, and is therefore always about to pass into zero.

It is this conception—not the watch or the telephone or the aeroplane—which is the cause of man's not having time. Time was lost to him metaphysically long before he had overcome it technically. The exact time-signal on the radio, which every decent citizen notes in order to set his watch correct to the second, the wrist watch, which at any moment shows him the exact time—all these devices have been invented because man wants them, because time vanishes under his fingers, because he does not have time any longer. We have reached here the opposite pole from the Oriental view. Reality is pulverised temporality. It is in vain that Faust wishes to see that moment to which he can say: "Verweile doch, Du bist so schön!" It is in vain that Nietzsche exclaims in a superb poem: "Denn alle Lust will Ewigkeit, will tiefe, tiefe, Ewigkeit". If once you have declared your option for the moment, the fate of your reality as radical temporality is determined, and radical temporality is vanishing time. Time dwindles away, constantly approaching zero.

It is for this reason that modern man wants to snatch as much of this time as possible, to get as much "into his time" as he can. He begins, so to say, a race with time, and in this race man is inevitably the loser, because it is the last moment which decides, and the last moment is death. Man races death, but death wins. Over the whole of life there looms this certainty of a lost race with death. But no one likes to face it. The thought of it is avoided, because man's chances are so absolutely hopeless. Modern man puts out of sight as well as he can all reminders of death; he does not want to hear of it, because the thought reminds him of his being the loser. All the same, the remembrance of death stands behind him with its whip like a slave-driver and urges him on. This—and this—and this I must have, cries man, before it is too late, before the door closes for ever. It is the panic of the closed door. This panic explains many of the features which are typical of modern life: man's hasty enjoyment, his all-dominating craving for security, to which finally he sacrifices freedom and his soul.

The Christian understanding of time and its relation to eternity stands midway between, but also above and beyond, the opposing views of East and West. At first sight it seems much more similar to the Eastern than to the Western concept, its main thesis being that God is eternal, and that therefore true reality is eternity. Is not the Gospel the promise of eternal life? Is it not said that God is unchangeable? "With Him there can be no variation, neither shadow that is cast by turning."[30] He is the same yesterday, to-day and in eternity. "For a thousand years in Thy sight are but as yesterday, when it is past." The time-process in its totality, from beginning to end, is present in Him. For Him there is no surprise. Everything that happens does so according to His eternal decree. God is eternal.

But the relation of this eternal God to temporal being and becoming is totally different from what it is in Indian thought or in the systems of Parmenides, Plato or the Neoplatonists. God creates the time, He *gives* time. As He, the Almighty, gives man room for his freedom, so He creates time for him, for his becoming and for his free action. Temporality is not an approach to nothingness any more than the created world is unreal. God has created time together with the world, He has set a beginning to time and will set an end of time. He gives every man his time, with a beginning and an end to his temporal existence, but the end of time and the beginning are not the same. The time-process does not come back to its beginning. Between these two points, the start and the finish, something happens, which even for God is real and significant. There is history, an individual and a universal human history, in which God is infinitely interested. He is so intensely concerned with this history that He not only looks down on the scene of human life like an interested spectator, but He Himself intervenes in it. Even more, at a certain point in this time-process, He Himself enters the scenery of temporal life; He, the eternal, appears in the shape of a historical person and, as such, performs, once and for all, the decisive act of all history. The incarnation of the word of God is at once the insertion into time of the eternal God: "When the fulness of time came, God sent forth His son ".[31] And in Him He revealed unto us the eternal secret of His will.[32]

This event charges the time of man's history with an extreme tension.[33] It is the time of expectation of the end, that end which is not the closed door, but the open door. It is the expectation of fulfilment. Time conceived in that fashion is the time of decision and probation. It is that time in which the eternal fate of the individual is decided. Therefore this sense of time is as remote from Oriental indifference to the temporal as from that time-panic of the modern Westerner. It is of the utmost significance, because it is within time that everything is decided for us, and every moment is a moment of decision. In every moment we have to keep faith; the servants must be awake all the time, for they do not know the day and the hour when the Lord comes; they do know, however, that if the Lord finds them sleeping they are lost, and that it will be said to them, as to those foolish virgins battering in vain on the closed door of the wedding-feast, "I know you not ".[34]

All the same, in spite of the tremendous tension and the weight of decision involved, this temporality is not the ultimate reality; it is an intermezzo between divine election in the beginning and eternal perfection beyond time, beyond the limit of death, beyond this historical movement.

These two aspects of time enable us to understand the Christian concept of history. As has often been observed, neither in Oriental nor in classical Greek thought does the problem of history play any rôle. For the Oriental as well as for the Greek—and, we may say, for all humanity outside of Biblical revelation—the image of temporal happening is that of the circle. Temporality, as far as it has any reality and any significance, is a circular movement, always returning on itself. It is the same movement which we observe in nature: day and night, summer and winter, birth and death in perpetual rotation. This movement, then, has no climax; it leads nowhere. It is therefore not worth while making it a problem of thought. This is why Greek philosophy, to which everything else has become a problem, never made history an object of philosophic reflection.

The theme of history as a topic of thought is Judeo-Christian, brought into our consciousness by the Old Testament prophets and by the New Testament Gospel. Here history is no circular movement. History is full of new things, because God works in it and reveals Himself in it. The historical time-process leads somewhere. The line of time is no longer a circle, but a straight line, with a beginning, a middle and an end. This is so because —if I may use a simile—God Himself has entered this circular time at a certain point, and with His whole weight of eternity has stretched out this time-circle and given the time-line a beginning and an end, and so a direction. By this incarnation or "intemporation" of the word of God, time has been charged with an immense intensity. It has become, as we have said, the time of waiting, of decision and probation. Thus history has become interesting as a theme even for the thinker. It is now worth while for a thinker of the highest calibre, like St. Augustine, to write his *De Civitate Dei* as a kind of Christian philosophy of history, in fact the first philosophy of history ever written.[35]

We have been speaking of the tension of temporality. Comparing, however, the Christian existence with that of the panic-stricken modern man, we could also speak of a removal of tension. " For I am persuaded, that neither death nor life . . . nor things present, nor things to come . . . shall be able to separate us from the love of God, which is in Christ Jesus our Lord."[36] " For I reckon that the sufferings of this present time are not worthy to be compared with the glory which shall be revealed in us."[37] Christian man, through his faith in Christ Jesus, is time-superior, time-exempt; he lives already in the coming eternity. Important as earthly events may be in his life and that of other men, the all-important, the true decision has already been made in Christ, and the believer's life consists only in living on the basis of this earlier decision. This is what is meant by " Living by faith ".

The Christian conception of time, then, permits and even obliges us to partake in temporal happenings with the utmost intensity—the picture presented by the New Testament being usually that of an athlete on the race-course, spending his last energy to reach the goal—and at the same time to be free from the haste and over-excitement created by the panic of the closed door. Those who live in faith are seriously intent on something going forward on this earth, something being bettered, so that the will of the Creator may be more fully expressed in His creation than it is now, under the domination of evil. But at the same time the life-feeling of the Christian is not dependent on whether or not this earthly goal is reached. He knows that whatever he can do for the realisation of God's will is at best something relative. He knows that whatever goes on within this temporality is encircled by the limits of death and fragility. And yet this insight into the insurmountable barrier does not make him resigned. His true, ultimate hope is not based on what can be achieved within temporal history, but upon that realisation of the divine purpose, which is neither dependent on man's action, nor happens within time, but sets an end to the temporal world, and which is not *a* goal, but *the* goal, the ultimate τέλος, the perfection of all things, which God gives and effects in bringing about life eternal.

The Christian understanding of history and its goal is sharply distinct from the idea of progress and evolution, which is characteristic of our era. Such a concept of universal evolution is unknown not only in the Eastern world but also in the West, so far as regards antiquity, the Middle Ages, and the period from the Reformation right up to the 18th century. Where the totality of temporal reality is interpreted by the symbol of a circle, there is no room for the idea of universal progress. Neither Heraclitus' πάντα ῥεῖ, nor Aristotle's entelechy means anything like a directed time-process. The stream of happenings of which Heraclitus speaks is a movement without direction and goal, an eternal fluctuation comparable to the moving sea. But neither does Aristotle's entelechial movement have any reference to history. It is an eternal movement without beginning or end. No Greek thinker ever conceived the Cosmos in such a way that it represents a movement in time directed towards a goal, so that the later generations of time are somehow better off than the previous ones. If there is anything like a universal direction in this time-process, it is a movement downwards rather than upwards, a decline or degeneration rather than an evolution or progress. Such is the mythical concept of the successive world-epochs, as we find it in Hesiod, and a similar consequence might be drawn from Neoplatonic metaphysics.

The idea of evolution is, however, also entirely unknown within early Christianity. It is true that the basic conception of the coming kingdom of God includes the idea of a goal of history. It is also true that within this historical, temporal world a hidden germ of this kingdom of God is growing, intensively and extensively. Still, the idea of universal progress is impossible within this Christian conception because, alongside this growth of the kingdom, there is the concurrent growth of the evil powers and their influence within this temporal world. The tares are growing together with the wheat.[38] The opposition to the kingdom is growing at the same rate as the kingdom itself, so that the later generations are in no way better off than the earlier ones. On the contrary—it is in the last days that the conflict between good and evil forces reaches a climax. The goal of history is reached not by an immanent growth or progress, but by a revolutionary change of the human situation at the end of history, brought about not by man's action, but by divine intervention—an intervention similar to that of incarnation, namely the παρουσία, the advent of the Lord, the resurrection of the dead, the coming of the eternal world. That this end of human history is utterly distinct from continuity and immanent growth is most clearly expressed in the idea of the *dies irae,* the day of the Last Judgment, which puts an end to human history. The framework of this Universe is broken, death—" the last enemy ", and the characteristic feature of the temporal world—is overcome and annihilated, and the eternal world is established. There is no room in this picture for the idea of universal progress and evolution.

On the other hand, the popular belief that the idea of evolution and progress was first worked out within natural science, and thence affected the conception of history, is false. The reverse is true: the idea has been transplanted from an evolutionary conception of history into natural science. Lamarck and Darwin are not the pioneers but the heirs of this modern idea. The real pioneers are men like Rousseau, Lessing, Herder, Hegel. The idea of progress and evolution is a child of the optimistic philosophy of the Enlightenment.

Its basis is an optimistic evaluation of human nature and, as its negative consequence, the repudiation of the fundamental Christian ideas of the Fall and of original sin. Human nature as such is good; at least, it is raw material fit to be shaped into something good, into true humanity. This anthropology seems to be based not on axiomatic speculation but on observation, on facts. History does begin with primitive man; he is the raw material out of which perfect humanity can be shaped. He it is whose mental capacities are not yet developed, whose cultural life has not yet begun. Civilisation and culture are acquired only in the course of a process extending through thousands of years, growing from generation to generation. It is this undeniable fact of the continuous growth of the benefits of civilisation, and of a progressive use of man's mental capacities, which is the backbone of the 18th-century idea of the universal progress of humanity.

This idea, however, is possible only by using a very dubious equation, *i.e.* the supposition that the more developed human life is in the cultural sense, the more human or good it is in the ethical sense; that moral evil is therefore only the primitive, the not-yet-developed; and that the good, the truly human is identical with the no-longer-primitive, the developed. Or—to express the same from the negative angle—the idea of universal progress is made possible only by denying the Christian conception of evil as sin, *i.e.* egoistic self-will and self-affirmation contradicting and opposing the will of God and the moral law. According to the Christian conception, there is continuity between the primitive state of mind and the developed one, but between the morally good and the morally evil there is no continuity but merely contradiction. Moral evil, understood as sin, is not that which is not yet good, but that which is no longer good. Sin is not undeveloped good, but spoilt and perverted good. It is not something which is not yet there, but it is a present reality of a negative character, the antagonism of men's will to the will of God. It is therefore only by substituting for the contradiction, for the Yes-and-No relation, the merely relative contrast of less and more, that the idea of universal progress is possible. As a consequence, the Christian idea of redemption is replaced by the idea of cultural development. The more man is trained to use his mental faculties, the more he gains power over the outside world and over his own forces, the more human he becomes, so the more evil disappears. This is the basic illusion of this favourite and most influential idea of modern man.

But where did 18th-century philosophy get the idea of a goal towards which history moves—an idea which was utterly foreign to rational philosophy in pre-Christian times? The answer, I think, is obvious, and the proof for it can easily be found in thinkers like Lessing and Herder. The idea of a universal goal of history is a Christian heritage, although completely transformed in context. Whilst, in the Christian view of history, this goal is transcendent in character, namely the world of resurrection and eternal life, it has now become immanent, being here identified with an imaginary terminus of the movement which leads from the primitive to civilised cultural life. In this fashion was formed that inspiring—not to say intoxicating—idea of idealistic progressivism which has taken hold of the best minds since the middle of the 18th century. It is the bastard offspring of an optimistic anthropology and Christian eschatology. Humanity as a whole is involved in a unique process, leading upwards from primitive beginnings, from a more or less animal start, to the loftiest peaks of true spiritual humanity, a process which is far from being finished, in which our generation is involved; one which perhaps will never be finished, but the end of which we are steadily approaching.[39]

It is this idea of evolution which modern natural science inherited and which it had only to supplement, to support and substantiate by its own means. From this idealistic conception Lamarck, Lyell and Darwin drew their ideas of an all-embracing evolution of life on this globe. The scientific evolutionism of the later 19th century is composed of two elements: this idealistic idea of progress, combined with certain observations in the field of biology. What 18th-century philosophy had worked out in the limited field of human history was now brought into a much larger context. The history of the forms of organic life on our planet seemed to corroborate such an optimistic idea of a universal development. Was it not a fact that everywhere the primitive, undifferentiated forms precede the differentiated, the higher forms or organisation? Therefore it would appear that life is moving onward to unknown heights. Again, it was not seen that this naturalistic form of evolutionism is based on an unjustified identification, namely that the more "differentiated" in the biological sense is the "higher" in the human or spiritual sense.

But, once taken for granted, this idea of evolution seemed to give a new value to temporal becoming, which in the thought of the ancient world was a merely negative concept. In the course of becoming the perfect seems to emerge gradually.[40] The splendour of the idea of perfection, which in ancient philosophy had been identified with the transcendent and timeless world of ideas, and which in Christian thought had been reserved for the divine, supernatural sphere, then seemed to have shifted over to the historical world and to natural forces. From then on it seemed to be possible to believe in perfection on the basis of purely secular, natural, even material, principles. Since the idea of progress had come into the wide field of natural science, it seemed to have become independent of all metaphysical and religious presuppositions. It had become an instrument of natural explanation.

This was certainly not the conception of Rousseau, Lessing, Herder and Hegel. When they were speaking of evolution, they meant something which was at the same time immanent and transcendent, natural and divine. For them evolution was not merely a causal process of differentiation, but in the literal sense an evolution, *i.e.* the disclosure of something divine hidden in the natural. To them the time-process was at once both natural and supernatural and certainly, in any case, teleological and spiritual, not merely causal and material. But with Darwin's theory of selection, teleology seemed to be superseded. The one principle of causality was sufficient not only to explain a process as such, but to explain a progress, *i.e.* a process with a certain definite direction. Now it was possible to have finality without a principle of finality, to have teleology on the basis of causality, to have a direction of history by merely natural forces —in a word, automatic progress.

This new phenomenon—the idea of evolution and progress— is not only important from the point of view of becoming, but also as an element in that feature which we found so character- istic of our age, the temporalisation of existence. By means of the idea of evolution it seemed possible to repudiate eternity and still keep all those values which in previous times had been con- nected with the eternal. The eternal·is no more necessary to give meaning to life. Temporal life, interpreted in terms of evolution, had meaning, direction and finality in itself. For that reason evolutionism became one of the most potent factors of temporalisation, of radical repudiation of the idea of eternity within the conception of human existence.

But I am constrained to offer some observations which lead to a different conclusion:—

1. Even granted that the idea of universal progress is correct—which we never should admit—it is undeniable that the result of this progress means very little to the individual. One has to think in generations, in centuries. This means that the interest moves away from the personal to the collective. The individual and his fate, his future, become irrelevant. It is only the totality which counts; or rather it is an abstract humanity forming, so to say, the subject of this evolution.

2. Therefore this present existence has no meaning and value of its own. It is merely a point of transition, a rung on the ladder which leads upward. Its own value—if you ask for such estimate—must be left indefinite, and is therefore open to question

3. But these factors lead in the direction which we have been calling the dwindling-away of time. The real, existing man appears to himself like a snapshot, a fraction of a large reel of film—a picture which, taken by itself, is as meaningless as a single frame cut from a movie strip and as absurd as a slow motion film. So this idea of evolution must—once its first intoxicating effect is over—take the whole substance away from life. It means that life is, as it were, eaten away from the inside.

Needless to say, this idea of a universal progress of such a natural upward movement is irreconcilable with Christian faith. This does not mean that the Christian cannot acknowledge certain aspects of the evolutionary theory of natural science. From the point of view of Christianity, there is no reason to deny that life on earth has a long history, spanning millions of years; that it has passed through many transformations; that the origins of mankind lie far back in prehistoric, primitive beginnings, presumably in animal forms. Within the limits which conscientious scientists have set for themselves, the evolutionist theory is not in conflict with Christian faith.

Two elements of this evolutionist thought, however, must be unconditionally rejected from the Christian point of view: first, the identification of moral evil or sin with the primitive; and, second, the assumption that the development of human intelligence, technical skill and cultural enrichment mean in themselves a progress in the sense of the truly human. The Christian conception of man includes the belief that the higher differentiation of intellectual powers, as well as the increase of the means of civilisation, is most ambiguous with regard to goodness and to the truly human. It can mean an increase of moral evil, of destructive inhumanity, just as much as the opposite. Civilised man, with the highest scientific and technical training, and commanding the accumulated wealth of ages of civilised life, may still be morally bad, even devilish, and if he is, he is so much the more dangerous. The highly developed human mind and the highly developed human civilisation may come to a point where they are capable of destroying all gains and goods in one frantic moment of diabolical madness.

This is why the modern identification of the idea of progress with the Biblical message of the kingdom of God is a demonstrable error which has most fatal effects. The idea of progress means a movement from here to there, from below to above, reaching more or less steadily towards a point in the far future, in which perfection is conceived of as materialised. The Christian message of the coming kingdom, however, means just the opposite movement—a movement coming down from above to below, from " heaven ", i.e. from the transcendent, to earth. Where it reaches the historical plane, it breaks the framework of this temporal, earthly existence. That is what is meant by resurrection, parousia, eternal life. The New Testament knows nothing whatever of a kingdom of God which develops according to the idea of progress, slowly, immanently, from below upward. This so-called kingdom of God is simply an invention of the 19th century, read into the Bible, but not to be found there. It is a mixture of the New Testament message and modern evolutionism, out of which nothing good can come, but only illusion, disillusionment and final despair.

One last question has not yet been touched: From the point of view of Christian faith and hope, what is the result and value of the historical process? This question cannot be answered by a simple scheme. The Christian expectation of the coming kingdom first of all places everything historical under the radical negation of the divine judgment. All human history is flesh, taking the word in its Biblical sense. Therefore it is transient. From the texture of history the two dark threads of sin and death cannot be eliminated anywhere, from the beginning to the end. They belong to the picture of historic life. History in its process already performs part of this judgment upon its own creations. "Die Weltgeschichte ist das Weltgeriche." History devours its own children; whatever it brings forth passes away some day. This, however, is only one side of the picture. There is also continuity, there is tradition, there is historical heritage. Not every epoch begins anew from nothing. We all live from the stored-up wealth of previous ages. Eternal life is not only the negation, but also the fulfilment of this earthly life. It is not only a new world, but also the perfection of this world. Even our body, which seems to be particularly perishable and unfit to inherit the eternal, will be not simply destroyed, but transformed into a completely obedient organ and expression of the life of the spirit.

If, however, we ask whether there is any part of this reality, any element of our present experience, which as such shall be deemed worthy to enter into the perfect eternal existence, the answer must be, Yes indeed, there is one element which, whilst being an experience within the Christian life, will also be *the* element of eternal life, namely love in the New Testament sense of Agapé. Neither the State, nor culture and civilisation, nor even faith and hope, are that element which remains in eternity, but love alone. For God Himself is Love. That is why it is said that whilst all other things pass away, including faith, knowledge, language and hope, love alone remains, and this love is the principle of true humanity.

V

THE PROBLEM OF MEANING

IF we ask what is the most urgent and burning problem engaging Western man in our time, the answer cannot be in doubt. What disquiets and torments him most is the problem of the meaning of life. What is the meaning of human existence? Has it any meaning at all? The terrific convulsions of this generation, which have laid open to question not only the survival of human civilisation but also the existence of the human race itself, together with the earthquake in the spiritual foundations of life, give this question an urgency and a radical character which it never had before nor ever could have had. But beyond this, the point has already been reached where man is so much inclined to doubt the meaning of life that he does not even put the question, and therefore sinks into a sub-human form of existence. So long as the problem of meaning is alive and burning, the spirit of man is alive. But where man ceases to ask this question, there the spirit is extinct. Man jumps from one experience to another, just as a squirrel leaps from branch to branch, and the oneness of his life is dissolved. It is in asking the meaning of life that man becomes aware of the totality of this existence.

Meaning is totality, wholeness. If we say, "This word has a meaning", what we are trying to say is that these different sounds or letters forming a word become one word through a spiritual unity, which binds them together and makes them intelligible. If we say that a phrase, a speech, a book, a work has a meaning, we are pointing again to the spiritual unity which ties the parts into a whole. It is in this fashion that the Greeks formed the concept or idea of Logos, implying by that word what we call meaning. They called it that because it was in human speech (Logos) that the character of spiritual unity or wholeness had struck their minds. Speech is the immediate manifestation of meaning.[41]

It is possible to approach the problem of meaning from another angle, which may be more familiar to modern man, namely from the angle of purpose. To forge a hammer, to build a house, or to plough the field has a meaning, because this action serves a definite purpose. This purpose, which gives meaning to action, is primarily a biological one: self-preservation, the preservation of race, nourishment, safeguarding physical existence. All these actions, which support the natural instinct of life-preservation in its spontaneous utterances, and which therefore place intelligence at the service of life-preservation, have a meaning, because they serve an obvious purpose. But the mental action which is placed at the service of vital necessities is not that which is distinctive for human life. The spiritual stands here under the domination of animal nature and merely completes what the natural instinct of the animal desires. The specifically human comes to the fore only where man does something which goes beyond the realm of physical preservation, whether it be by the way in which it is done—eating, instead of feeding, building houses, instead of creeping into holes—or by the fact that goods are created or spiritual actions performed which serve higher requirements than the necessities of life. The meaning of human life therefore must become visible where human action is not under the domination of natural urge but of spiritual purposes. Where we have in mind such purposes, the two concepts " meaning " and " purpose " merge into each other. The animal has merely vital purposes, but man has such purposes as have meaning in themselves and which, as such, give his life its specific human stamp. It is in things or actions which have their unity in their spiritual purpose that the spirit expresses itself as the unifying power.

Meaning is therefore a fundamental factor of culture and civilisation. Nay, one can even say that culture is materialisation of meaning. Culture is the creation of units which exist only for the spirit. For the dog there is no Rembrandt picture, but only specks of colour, no Beethoven symphony, but merely a series of noises or perhaps tones. The spirit is the meaning-creating and meaning-acknowledging power, and culture is the totality of meaning-creating powers and meaningful creations of man. But culture or civilisation taken by itself cannot in itself answer the question of meaning, for the idea of meaning is curiously inexorable. Because it means totality, it cannot be satisfied with anything partial. The single work does not suffice, the spirit cannot but ask for the totality of all works, of all human doing. Just as one cannot be satisfied with the single meaningful word, but only by the meaningful connection of single meaningful words through the spiritual unity of a speech as a whole, or a book as a whole, so the spirit in seeking for meaning demands the unity of man's life as a whole. Not even the unity of all man's action is sufficient, because man's action is in relation with something else—with nature, with the world in which it is performed and with which it is wrestling by thought and action. For that reason the mind, wherever it is truly living, cannot but ask for a total meaning, and it is through the intensity of this question that the aliveness of the spirit manifests itself. Where this question of total meaning ceases to be asked, the spirit is in a state of disintegration, and human life is about to perish in a sub-human, animal existence.

That is why men have always asked for the meaning of life, for a total meaning. They sought the answer in their religions or their philosophies. The religious myths are to be understood, in the last analysis, as attempts to interpret the ·total meaning of existence. In the same way philosophy, in its truly great and powerful forms, has to be evaluated as an attempt to discover meaning by the use of rational thought; as the Greeks said, λόγον διδόναι. Here it is possible only to sketch a few of these attempts. In Indian religion, the problem of the meaning of life was answered by the doctrine of Karma—the circle of birth or the transmigration of souls—and in the body of doctrines teaching man how to get out of this circle of birth and to enter Nirvana. These answers rested upon the presupposition that this empirical existence, as such, is not meaningful, but that, on

the contrary, meaning consists in living and thinking in such a
way as to escape from this life. With regard to this life, then,
the answer is thoroughly pessimistic.

Another solution of the problem, impressive in itself, is the
ethical dualism of the religion of Zarathustra. The meaning of
life consists in supporting life and defending it against everything which destroys and kills it. Here, also, the truly
significant thing it not life, as such, but eternal, imperishable
life, which one achieves by following that rule. By joining
battle with the good god in his fight against the god of destruction, man gets his share in the victory of the good god
and his eternal life. Apart from the answer of the Christian
Gospel, however, the most important solution of the problem of
meaning within Western history is that of Greek philosophy.
Of course, as we all know, this philosophy is not a unity, but
presents itself in a variety of very different systems. But within
our Western history, it was primarily Greek idealism—this word
taken in a very broad sense—which became influential. The
meaning-giving principle of this philosophy is the divine Nous
or Logos, which permeates the world and forms it into a
Cosmos. It is the same Logos which underlies meaningful
speech and thought as well as all cultural activity of man. Man's
speech and action are meaningful in so far as they partake of this
divine Logos. The divine Logos, then, is seen in closest connection with the logical or rational element of our life. This
relation to the divine Logos appears in the various systems of
Greek philosophy—of Plato, of Aristotle, of the Stoics, and
the Neoplatonists, in different settings, according as they placed
the emphasis more on the secular, the cultural, scientific,
artistic or philosophical element, or on the ethical and religious
aspect of human life. They all have in common this reference
to the divine Logos or the ideas, as that which contains the
meaning, and are therefore akin to each other in a marked
rational and immanentist tendency. It is the divine reason,
immanent in our reason and in our reasonable doing and
thinking, upon which the meaning of life is grounded.[42]

Within the Christian doctrine and faith the principle of

meaning, *i.e.* that which gives meaning to our existence, can be summarised also by the word Logos. We recall the pregnant and, at the same time, cryptic words of the Prologue to St. John's Gospel: " In the beginning was the Logos, and the Logos was with God and the Logos was God. The same was in the beginning with God. All things were made by Him; . . . In Him was life; and the life was the light of men . . ." etc. No doubt it is this Logos in which the whole world has its meaningful foundation as well as its meaningful end, in which therefore the meaning of human life is mysteriously contained. But this Logos is not the Logos of Greek philosophy; there are three radical differences between the two. The first is that it is not an abstract principle, an " it ", as it always is in Greek philosophy, but a person—" in *Him*, all things were made by *Him* and in *Him* was life ". The second is to be seen in the fact that this Logos is not an immanent element of the human mind or spirit, but given to man by historical revelation as the secret of God's essence and will. Finally, it is not a timeless, fixed truth, but the moving dynamism of history, the definite manifestation of that which in the end of time brings with it the victory of the divine will over the powers that threaten the meaning of life, and which perfects historical revelation in eternal life, thus completing the meaning of historical, earthly existence.

It might appear, at first glance, that this conception of meaning would be closely related to that of Persian dualism, which we have just been sketching. As a matter of fact, certain common traits as well as certain historical connections between the two cannot be denied.[43] All the same, there is an unfathomable gulf between them. One should not over-emphasise the difference between the Christian conception and the element of metaphysical dualism in the conception of Zarathustra. For this dualism, after all, manifests itself as being less than ultimate by the certain victory of the good god over the evil spirit. The opposition between the two lies somewhere else, namely in the fact that in Biblical revelation the idea of God's mercy, His redeeming grace and love, is central and dominating, whilst it is entirely absent in the religious system of Zarathustra. Here it is the good men who, by the proof of their moral sincerity, acquire participation in the final victory and eternal life, whilst in the Christian Gospel it is the sinners, graciously pardoned and saved by the atoning sacrifice of Christ and God's merciful forgiveness, who become participants in eternal life and thereby in the completion of meaningfulness. It is therefore not to be wondered at that within Christian history and Western history at large, the Persian solution of the problem does not play any conspicuous rôle. The discussion is primarily between the Biblical revelation on the one hand, and Greek idealism on the other.

This discussion between the two predominant principles of meaning within our history—between the Greek Logos-principle and the Biblical revelation of the Logos-Son, of Jesus Christ—marks the beginning of the modern epoch. From the end of classical antiquity up to this point, the Christian idea had been entirely dominant, although not in its original purity. Modern spiritual history, on the other hand, is characterised primarily by a progressive displacement of the Christian, the transcendent, revelatory, personalistic conception of meaning, by an immanent, rational and abstract principle. Human reason sets itself on its own feet. It thinks itself capable of solving the problem of meaning from its own resources. That is why European thought re-established its connections with the models of Greek philosophy. Of course, this could not be done without thorough-going modifications and variations. Two essential traits, however, remained in common between the modern and the Greek conceptions of meaning: the predominance of the rational, logical element and the tendency towards an immanent solution. Meaning must prove itself in its rationality, and the realisation of meaning must take place within this temporal existence. This limitation necessarily produced, in recent centuries, the new idea so characteristic of our epoch, about which we have already spoken in the last lecture: the idea of progress.[44]

If rationality on the one hand and this historical existence on the other are to be sufficient to answer the question of the meaning of life, it is necessary either to prove this existence to be rational, or to show the possibility of believing in rationality, in spite of the present irrational character of existence. The first of these two ways is that of Theodicy, *i.e.* the proof that what exists is at least approximately rational; it was possible only (as we see in its greatest example—that of Leibnitz) as long as it was possible to draw considerably from the Christian theological tradition. It is therefore no mere chance that as soon as this method—the Leibnitzian Theodicy—lost its power of conviction, the second began to be taken.[45] The death of Leibnitz coincides almost exactly with the appearance of the idea of progress, first in the form of an idealistic, speculative philosophy of history, later in the form of a naturalistic, pseudo-scientific evolutionism.

Those who had broken with the religious faith of the Christian tradition and were still seeking a meaning for existence, could certainly not be expected to find that rational meaning within the given realities of the natural and cultural life of their time. The elements of negation and destruction of meaning were too obvious even for the most optimistic rationalist to ignore them. From this difficulty the idea of progressive evolution seemed to afford an escape. This world is *not yet* rational and therefore meaningful, but it can and it *shall become* so. How is it possible for it to become rational? The answer was: It can and will become more and more rational by a progressive spiritualisation of nature and human life in the course of cultural expansion; by a progressive elimination of what is really or seemingly irrational, by rational action and rational thought, therefore by a double evolution of the powers of divine reason immanent in man through his action and his thought. It was this idea of a spiritual evolution and the progressive elimination of irrational elements by cultivating and educating the individual, by extensive and intensive increase of cultural and civilising action, as well as by progressive knowledge, which gave the last two centuries their dynamic *élan* and their feeling of assurance.

It was inevitable, however, that in the course of this movement the tendency towards this-worldliness became more and more conspicuous and predominating. The high-minded, idealistic evolutionism of Herder, Humboldt, Schleiermacher and Hegel gave way increasingly to a more realistic and earth-bound principle of progress, which was related more closely to the interest of the average man, and was also more credible than the idea of a progressive spiritualisation of the world. As the stream of idealistic enthusiasm began to decline, its place was taken by the more prosaic idea of scientific and technical progress, of the spread of democratic freedom, and of overcoming irrationality by raising the level of general education. In all these fields progress was conspicuous to everybody. Moreover, it was in close relation to the practical interest and everyday life of the large majority of men. The surprising and truly revolutionary achievements of technical industry, the no less astounding progress of natural science, the rapid spread of democratic institutions and of general education seemed to justify this belief in progress so completely as to place it beyond doubt. Mankind became intoxicated by these visible and indubitable manifestations of progress, in the sphere of its practical needs, to such an extent that there seemed to be no room or capacity left to meditate seriously on the profound problem of life's meaning. All those things which threaten the meaningfulness of man's life—death, evil, suffering—all these voices were drowned by the loud-speaker of progressivism.

This optimism, threatened by the truly irrational social conditions, which had actually been created by the revolutionary progress of technical industry, could be sustained only by the hope of a social paradise which Karl Marx preached as coming inevitably. But then came the time when this intoxication began to wear off, when it became more and more apparent that, in spite of all school education, men were not becoming better, that, in spite of all technical progress, life had not become more human, but on the contrary more and more inhuman. Above all, the disillusionment was hastened by the first great and the second even greater shock brought about by the first and the second world-wars, with their revelation of demoniac, even diabolic, backgrounds of human existence and human nature.

The belief in progress had played out its fatally dazzling rôle, and Western humanity, which had staked all its hope on this one card, found itself facing the nothingness of despair. Now, in view of the ruins of his civilisation, in uncertainty as to whether the past storm, which had destroyed in a few years what centuries had built, might not soon be followed by another even more terrible, which would mean the end of all civilisation, perhaps the end of humanity itself—now, faced by all this, mankind experiences the dawning of the fearful and disastrous thought that life probably has no meaning at all.

If, looking back from the standpoint of Christian faith, we ask ourselves why this has happened, and was bound to happen, it will not do to point merely to the last degenerate forms to which the idea of progress had fallen a prey, or in which an already decaying evolutionary creed expressed itself. It is not in these obvious and most recent extremes, but in the first spiritual and exalted beginnings that we have to discover the roots of the evil. We have to go back as far as Greek idealism, and its fundamental conception of the principle of meaning, in order to understand the completely nihilistic disappearance of meaning which has threatened our generation. The first thing we can observe, then, is that this idealistic principle of meaning was based entirely upon the " formal " side of the human mind. It is the possession of reason which distinguishes man from animal; it is reason by which man produces culture and civilisation; it is reason that links man to the divine. It is sufficient, it appears, that man has reason. Reasonable or spiritual action *as such* confers meaning. One does not ask *what* this reason thinks, what direction spiritual activity takes; it is the *possession* of reason in itself that makes man human and links him to the divine. Reason, as such, is the divine. You can find this same idea even nowadays in the speeches and writings of eminent spiritual leaders, repeated and varied a hundred times: " We believe in the spirit, in reason, in the human mind as that which gives life meaning and makes man human ".

From the Christian point of view, this idea can be seen as a great illusion. Human reason as such, spiritual activity as such, can be both good and evil, godlike and diabolical. There is a godlike and there is a godless use of reason. Therefore there is a possibility of culture being according to God, and also of its being quite godless. The possession of reason, of intellectual activity as such, is no guarantee of truth, goodness, and true humanity. The principle of the truly human, of goodness and truth is higher than reason. It does not lie within the sphere of the formal, not in a *that*, but in a *what*, not in the possession and use of spiritual powers, but in the right use, in the right relation, in the right decision, in that self-determination which is according to God's will.

The formalism of the idealistic principle of meaning is founded, as we have already seen, in a second factor, in the theological immanence-conception. Man is—that is the assumption here—partaker of divine nature by being a reasonable creature. The divine element is immanent in him because the divine element is in itself reason, the same reason which also dwells in him, in man's nature. Therefore, idealism cannot understand what we Christians assert, that evil is a spiritual thing, an act of reason and not of sensuality. For the idealist, evil is that which is divided from the spirit, emptiness, the reason-vacuum, therefore animal sensuality and brute instinct. The acknowledgment of the spiritual nature of evil would explode the whole philosophy of immanence. Therefore the idealist cannot but refuse to admit this conception of evil, and by doing so he is bound to minimise evil. Only that evil which is understood as spiritual is truly evil. What comes out of animal nature is not really evil: it is pre-moral primitivity.

Let us consider the same idea from a third point of view. The Greek idealistic conception of meaning is primarily taken from man's cultural activity. Indeed, culture is a primary manifestation of the meaningful; as we said before, culture is the materialisation of meaning. But, as we shall see more clearly later on, culture itself is primarily formal, because culture is the expression of a given spirituality or spiritual condition. Culture therefore is not in itself *the* human, but it is an instrument, an expression of the human; just as mind is not *the* human but the organ of the truly human. Culture is the expression of the given spiritual status, good or bad, human or inhuman, of a certain time or group. It is related to the truly human as the style of a speech or a book is related to its content. You can express truly diabolical ideas in the most superb style, and it can hardly be doubted that the devil, if he wants to be, is a very brilliant stylist. Therefore there can be false culture, just as much as false spirituality—even anti-human, godless culture. Culture, then, is not in itself the measure of humanity but merely the measure of the degree of spiritual intensity, whether good or bad. This misunderstanding which accepts culture as the criterion of humanity is, however, the fatal error of both ancient and modern idealism, and of modern thinking at large.

Now, this whole misunderstanding, implied in the Greek idealistic principle of God-immanence, stands in the closest relation to what the Bible calls sin. Man, understanding himself in that fashion, understands himself primarily as divine. He accepts as his nature what is in fact a divine *gift*. He wrongly assumes his rational nature to be the content instead of seeing it as a vessel. It is Hamann, the great Christian seer of the 18th century, who has called this " the misunderstanding of reason about itself ". He points to the origin of the German word " Vernunft ", which is derived from " vernehmen, annehmen ", " to receive ", and therefore expresses a relation of receptivity and dependence. True reason would be that which receives the divine, not that which thinks it *has* the divine in itself, or that it *is*, in its depth, the divine. True reason, then, would be only that which does not think it has the meaning of existence in itself but is ready to receive it from God. Greek idealism, in its pre-Christian form, remained in a measure religious, because it believed in the objectivity of the divine Logos. The idealism of modern times, however, having branched off from Christianity and left Christian truth behind, could not fail to become irreligious, and contained a dangerous element of rebellion which was lacking in the old Platonism. That is the fundamental reason why the emancipation from Christianity,

Read:

introduced and begun by modern idealism, ended in such meaninglessness."[46] *Good*

According to Christian faith, the meaning of life is not *in* man—neither in his rational nature nor in his rational or cultural work—but comes *to* him as a divine gift, as the Logos, which is the revealed Word, and as that Word which is the self-revealing God. Meaning, then, comes from transcendence, out of the mystery of divine being, the Logos, that (as the fourth Gospel says) " was in the bosom of the Father ".[47] This mystery does not remain in its transcendence; it reveals itself, it communicates itself. This Logos is the self-communicating Love of God, which in itself is personal being: the Son of Love. It is in Him, through Him, that human life receives its true humanity, its goodness and truth. " Grace and truth came by Jesus Christ."[48] Man's life receives this Word by an act which is mere reception—the act of faith—and this faith manifests its essence as being divine love by " working itself out in loving ".[49]

Now, in this fact—that man's life has no meaning in itself and in his own creation, but has to receive it—lies the possibility that the negative powers, death, evil, suffering, which threaten the meaning of life, can be regarded without palliation, without any attempt at theodicy, in their sheer, naked negativity. It is the Christian faith alone which makes no such attempt to extenuate evil, as is found, for instance, in the Neoplatonic idea that evil belongs to the good just as the contrast is necessary for harmony, or in the older Platonism in the identification of evil and animal instinct. No, evil is understood as sin; evil, understood as sin, means rebellion against the divine will, destruction of the good order of God, disintegration of the totality or wholeness of human life, hence, as the radical negation of meaning. Similarly, death is not glossed over as a mere fact of nature belonging to the Cosmic order; death also is ranked among the anti-divine powers threatening and destroying the meaning of life. Death is an " enemy " and not a friend. Because these two elements, sin and death, and the suffering issuing from them, determine the character of human life in such a fashion that nothing is untouched by them, no attempt is made to understand earthly existence in itself as meaningful. On the contrary, it is explicitly affirmed that this temporal existence, taken by itself, is meaningless, even contrary to meaning. And this applies to the total history of humanity as well as to that of the human individual. Historical life does not have meaning in itself. It acquires it from outside itself, and where this happens, there this earthly history comes to its end, there the new æon begins, life eternal.

It is, however, just the knowledge of this coming new existence which gives this earthly historical life a share of the eternal completion of meaning. To live in this hope by firm belief is no mere expectation, but is in itself the beginning of the ultimate realisation of meaning. For that divine love, which is the end of all things, is not a thing merely of the future, but it is a present reality for and in the believer. This love, Agapé, is the new principle of life of the Christian and the Christian community. The divine ultimate meaning, life in the Love of God, is present reality in faith, although imperfect and wrestling with those powers threatening the destruction of life and its meaning.

If we compare with this vision of historical reality, as it is given in Christian faith, the highest conception which the idea of meaning has acquired within a non-Christian interpretation— namely, within idealistic evolutionism—we see, quite apart from its unreality, the disguised resignation implicit in this idea of progress. The tremendous difference between the two is in the single fact that, whilst the Christian Gospel makes every believing individual a partaker of the ultimate perfection, the completion of meaning for the individual is most uncertain within any idealistic conception of history. Who, after all, has the profit of this infinite progressive movement? Every generation has to sacrifice itself, to place itself beneath the feet of the next generation, so as to raise it higher, merely in order to be in itself a mere step on the infinite road of humanity to a far-off, never attainable goal. But for me, as individual man, there is little enough consolation in the thought that those coming after me are a little nearer the goal, without reaching it themselves.

We need not bother any more about this tempting but illusory and fantastic idea of universal progress.   History itself has given judgment on it.   The negative powers of human nature, which threaten to destroy all the meaning of life, even the bare physical existence of humanity, have shown themselves with such naked brutality that the idea of universal progress as the solution of the problem of meaning is utterly discredited.   This fact can mean one of two things.   It can mean the lapse into complete despair about the meaning of life, resignation to the fact that there is no such meaning, that it is better not to ask this question at all but to content oneself with the fragmentary and transient glimpses of meaning, which are inherent in human life and activity.   Or it can mean that humanity turns its mind towards the Gospel as the only interpretation of existence, which is, at the same time, both realism without illusion and promise of fulfilment without resignation.

Two things must be said, however, about the Christian faith as solution of the problem of meaning in our time.   First, it is not easily come by.   Probably it never was.   But for centuries it had the advantage of being the accepted creed of the Western world.   Whether this was an advantage with respect to its true understanding can be doubted; it certainly had an important bearing on the formation of cultural stability and homogeneity.   But this is gone.   Christian faith has become, as it has never been since the first centuries of the Christian era, a matter of personal decision.   The second point is this.   Whilst Christian faith is the same at all times with respect to its foundation and content, it is different in every age as regards the frontier line along which it joins battle.   The frontier line of our age is neither that of the first centuries, which was marked by rival religions, nor is it that of the Middle Ages or that of the Reformation era, when it was marked by rival interpretations of its foundation and content.   In our time the frontier line is the alternative to a philosophy of despair, hidden in a number of more or less subtle evasions of the problem.[50]   Apart from these disguises, the question placed before man in our time is quite simple: Despair and pay the price of despair, or believe the Gospel and pay the price of believing!   What the price is of gaining the meaning of life, as the Gospel alone gives it, the Gospel makes clear enough. This must be added to what was said about the Christian conception of the meaning of life: such a conception cannot be gained by any theoretical argument. The Gospel will always be rejected when it is misunderstood as merely a satisfactory theory. To understand what it says about the meaning of life, and to see that this is the truth, is identical with that total change of the character and orientation of life which is implied in the words, repentance and faith. It is only in these acts that the Gospel-perspective can be won, and with it the solution of the problem of meaning.

VI

MAN IN THE UNIVERSE

WITH this lecture we enter the field of those questions which may be called problems of humanism or the humane. The first of these problems comes from without; it is raised for us by the universe in which we find ourselves. All humanism, whether of a Christian or idealistic type, draws its life from the conviction that man's position within this Cosmos is a distinctive and, indeed, a unique one, and that man has to vindicate against nature something which belongs to himself alone. All humanism gives man a place over, against and somehow outside of nature and elevates him above it. Therefore there is an inescapable either/or between this opposition of man and nature on the one hand, and on the other a conception of continuity which ranges man entirely with nature, and thus destroys the foundations of humanism. Humanism therefore, since it can be destroyed by a complete naturalism of this kind, is not a self-evident proposition.

Now it is curious that this nature-continuum, which denies the uniqueness of man and thereby sinks the human element in nature, stands at the beginning as well as at the end of the human history which we can survey. For the primitive mind there is no demarcation between man and surrounding nature. On the contrary, man and nature form one unbroken continuum. This appears primarily in the scheme by which primitive man interprets his relation to the animal. The totems of primitive tribes show that man believes in a real consanguinity between himself and certain animals, and thereby in a real descent of man from the animal world. Primitive man is, so to speak, a pre-scientific Darwinian, and the Darwinian of our time, by the same token, is a scientific primitive, if by Darwinism we understand a popular evolutionary philosophy rather than a strictly scientific hypothesis. There is, however, this considerable difference between the primitive and the modern nature-continuum, that in the world of primitive man the continuity is not established entirely at the cost of man. In the same measure that man is akin to the animal, the animal in its turn is akin to man. For the primitive mind, nature as a whole is somehow human. In this primitive world there are no "natural forces" in the present meaning of the word, but only forces which are at once of a personal and in some measure of a spiritual nature. Nature behaves in a way similar to man. You can talk with it, and it talks to you. All this is foreign to the conception of the modern Darwinist. Nature for him is conceived of as an object, *i.e.* it is radically non-personal. Nature is primarily a mechanism, and this is an idea entirely foreign to the primitive mind. The nature-continuum of modern times is established exclusively at the cost of man. Man has ceased to be something particular within a world which is conceived of in terms of mechanism. Therefore he is himself something like a highly-complicated mechanism. Whilst the primitive mind arrives at its scheme of continuity by the personification of nature, the modern mind arrives at it by a depersonification of man. It must now be our task to discover the background of this change in trying to summarise the history of man's thought about his place in the universe.

It is by a slow process that man has overcome the primitive nature-continuum. I would suggest that the best guide for the discovery of the history of human emancipation from nature is plastic art. The continuum is still living in all that mythological art which represents natural forces, understood as deities, in human shape as well as in animal—such art as we find in India as well as in old Egypt and Babylon. The decisive breach within this continuum happened in two distinct places: in Israel and in Greece. Leaving apart for the moment the Biblical concept of man, we may say that it is the unique contribution of the Greek mind to have abolished the animal shape of deity. In the mythological struggle of the Olympic gods against the

How about Persians? Confucius? Buddha?

semi- and totally bestial monsters, against the figures of the dark regions, there comes to the fore something of this unique inner liberation which takes place within the Greek conception of man. Man rises above the animal world; man becomes conscious of his uniqueness as a spiritual being distinct from a natural world.

But now, alongside this emancipation from and destruction of the nature-continuum, another process takes place, expressing itself again in plastic art, namely the *rapprochement* between deity and humanity which appears in an anthropomorphic deity and in the apotheosis of the human hero. This double process, first taking place in the subconscious forms of mythology, enters the full light of consciousness in philosophical reflection. Man discovers in himself that which distinguishes him from the animal and nature as a whole and elevates him above it, the Nous or the Logos, that spiritual principle which underlies all specifically human activity and gives man's work the character and content of human dignity. Now, this Nous or Logos is, at the same time, the principle which links mankind with the divine; the Logos is not merely the principle of human thought and meaningful action, but also that divine force which orders the world and makes it a Cosmos. It is the divine spark in human reason by which alone man emancipates himself from nature and places himself above it. It is that same divine spark in his reason in which he experiences the divinity of his innermost being. The continuum, then, is not broken, but shifted. Just as the divine Logos permeates nature and orders it, so it also permeates and orders man. But in man this divine principle becomes conscious knowledge. It is in the recognition of himself as partaker in the divine Logos that man becomes conscious of his specific essence and value; his humanity is, at the same time, divinity. This is the fundamental conception of Greek humanism in its conscious reflected form, freed from mythology.

In Biblical revelation the continuum of primitive mind is disrupted in an entirely different manner. A three-fold barrier is erected here: the barrier between God and the world, between God and man, and between man and nature. God is no more the immanent principle of the world, but its Lord and Creator.

He, the Lord-creator, alone is divine. Everything which is not Himself is creature, product of His will. Therefore He is opposite the world, His essence, His divine being, is other-than-world, He is the Holy One.[51] That is why He does not allow Himself to be depicted in any form: " Thou shalt not make unto thee any graven image nor any likeness of any thing that is in heaven above or that is in the earth beneath, or that is in the water under the earth ". But now—and this is the second barrier—it is not merely the nature-image of godhead which is forbidden to man, but equally the man-image. By that same character of holiness by which God is distinguished from nature, He is also distinguished from and placed opposite to man. Man, in spite of every thing he has and is, with all his spiritual as well as natural powers, is not divine. He is a creature. The barrier which separates God and the world also separates God and man.

All the same, in spite of this sharp separation from God, man is not placed on the same level as the rest of the world and not seen in continuity with nature.[52] Although man is not at all God, and God is not at all man, man is distinguished from all other creatures and elevated above them by a criterion of a specific kind. Man alone is created in the image of God. This likeness of man to God is the third barrier which is erected here. For man alone is created *in* the image and *to* the image of God. And this *imago dei* is the principle of Christian humanism as distinguished from Greek. At first sight it might appear as if this concept of *imago dei* meant something similar to the Greek idea that man is raised above the level of nature by his participation in the divine Nous or Logos dwelling in his reason. But the similarity between the two principles of humanism is merely apparent, for man's being created in the image of God does not imply any kind of divine spiritual substance in man, but only his relation to God. That which gives man his specific place in the Universe and specific dignity is not something which he has in his rational nature but his *relation* to the Creator. This relation is established by God's calling man to Himself and is realised by man's hearing this call and answering it by his own decision. That is to say, between God and man there exists the relation of calling and responsibility founded in the divine Word and man's faith, a faith which works through love.

Christian humanism therefore, as distinguished from the Greek, is of such a kind that the humane character of existence is not automatically a possession of man, but is dependent on his relation to God, and remains a matter of decision. The humane character of man is not guaranteed in advance like a natural disposition. It realises itself only in that answer of man which corresponds to the divine call. There is a possibility of its not realising itself but of being perverted through a false decision into an untrue inhumane humanity. Even more: not only can this happen, but it has actually happened. It is the case that man has made the wrong decision and has thereby lost his true humanity, and can regain it only by a new act of creation of God, by redeeming grace. However, even the man who has lost his true humanity has not altogether lost his distinctive human character. In spite of his wrong decision, he still is and remains within that primary relation of responsibility and therefore retains—if not the truly humane content—at least the structure of human being. He is still distinguished from the rest of creation by the fact that he, and he alone, is a responsible person. Furthermore, to this man who has lost his true humane character, God, by His revelation of divine redeeming love in the God-man, Jesus Christ, has offered the possibility of re-acquiring the true image of God; and, lastly, to those who accept this offer in obedient faith, the perfection and realisation of their eternal divine destiny is promised as the final goal of all history. That, in a few words, is the basis and content of Christian humanism.

Although the great difference between Christian and idealistic Greek humanism is quite obvious, they have at least this in common, that in both man is given a pre-eminent position in the Universe and is set over against and above nature on the sub-human level. In both man has a higher destiny, lifting him above the natural sphere and functions, and making him a par-taker of a divine eternal meaning. In both the *humanum* has a rich content and is distinctly separated from the animal world.

Therefore it is not surprising that where these two great streams of humanism met each other in history they did not merely flow alongside one another, but merged into one. Thus there was formed in the first centuries of our era something like a Christian-Greek or a Christian-idealistic humanism, a synthesis in which sometimes the classical, sometimes the Biblical element was predominant. But these two kinds of humanism were never clearly seen in their specific nature and so distinguished or separated from each other. It was only in the middle of the second millennium that a double-sided process of disentanglement or dissociation took place, on the one side from a genuinely Christian or Biblical conception of man, on the other side from a renewed classical idealistic humanism. The one we call Reformation, the other Renaissance.[53] In previous lectures we mentioned the fact that the spiritual history of recent centuries is on the whole characterised by a progressive emancipation from Biblical revelation and, hence, by a progressive domination of the rational element. The question which we have to answer is why this process led to a complete dissolution of humanism in the naturalist nihilism of our own day.

It is customary to answer this question by pointing to two epoch-making scientific discoveries, namely the revolutionary change within the conception of the spatial universe connected with the name of Copernicus, and that other no less revolutionary re-establishment of the nature continuum connected with the name of Darwin. There is no doubt that both the destruction of the geo-centric world picture and the expansion of the spatial world into the infinite, as well as the doctrine of the descent of man from animal forms of life, came as a tremendous shock to the generations which these discoveries took by surprise. But in both cases it has become clear that this shock was of a psychological rather than of a spiritual nature. For, if we contemplate these discoveries dispassionately, it becomes clear that, whilst they were bound to shake the frame of the traditional world-picture, they could not by their own truth destroy or even endanger the substance of humanism, whether Christian or idealistic.

In defending themselves against unconsidered consequences drawn from these discoveries, idealistic and Christian humanism have a common interest. They have to make clear the difference between the results of scientific research and the false interpretation of these results by a naturalistic philosophy. The Copernican destruction of geo-centricism could, if I may use the phrase, be easily digested both by Christian and idealistic humanism. For, after all, what has the assertion of the independence and superiority of man over nature to do with the quantitative extension of the spatial world or with the destruction of an astronomical geo-centricism? That man, quantitatively considered, is a mere nothing in the Universe was known before Copernicus and often found expressed in the language of Homer as well as in that of the Old Testament. To anyone who understands that the human character of existence is no matter of quantities, but of quality, the multiplication of man's quantitative disproportion with the Universe, involved in the new cosmology, cannot make any difference. No one has given clearer expression to this fundamental perception than Kant, in calling his idealistic philosophy a reversal of the Copernican revolution.[54] As the knowing subject, man stands above the world which is his object, whether it has the lines of the ancient or of the modern picture of the world. In a similar fashion, Christian theology, knowing that man's eminence is based upon God's call in His revelation, understands without difficulty that this revelation is not tied up with an astrophysical geo-centricism. For those to whom it seems difficult to separate these two points of view, it may be comforting to hear that modern astrophysics has, as Eddington pointed out,[55] established a new kind of geo-centrism, based on the observation that it is highly improbable that there are other celestial bodies besides our earth furnishing the conditions for the development of organic life and therefore of something like human existence. The earth, then, seems to have an exceptional place even in the modern world-picture. If, however, one likes to conceive of reasonable beings independent of organic substance, it would not be difficult to relate such a view to the Biblical concept of an angelic world. However this may be, the Copernican discovery and its enlargement in modern astrophysics cannot legitimately be regarded as a serious danger for any kind of humanism.

The case of Darwinism seems more dangerous. Granted that the hypothesis of the descent of man from animal forms of life has become a scientifically established fact—whether this is the case or not, science alone can decide and seems as yet not to have decided definitely—does this not mean that the continuity between man and animal is established and therefore that man has lost any claim to an exceptional position? If this were so, this would no doubt mean that humanism has lost its basis. The human would be nothing but a transformation of the animal. There would be no independence or superiority of the spiritual, humane element, no possibility of speaking of "higher" and "lower" in a qualitative or normative sense. Man would be nothing but a more differentiated animal, and ethics nothing but a form of natural instinct for the preservation of the race. But once again dispassionate contemplation of the facts and their implications shows that to draw such a consequence from the zoological data is entirely illegitimate. The specifically human can never be derived from the animal, even if it is true that the specifically human element begins to appear in such a minimal form that its distinction from the animal is difficult. After Darwin, just as before him, there is between man and animal the same unbridgeable gulf, included in the concepts of spirit, culture, responsible personality. A concept *is* different from associated sensations; a logical or ethical norm *is* different from a fact of nature; culture and civilisation *are* something different from satisfying biological impulses; responsible personality *is* different from affective individuality. If man as *zoon* is a mere species of the family of mammals, he is as *humanus* different from all animals and from all nature by just those elements which make up the *humanum*. Man alone produces cultural life: this is the argument of idealistic humanism. Man alone can hear the word of God: this is the argument of Christian humanism. It is not science, but an unconsidered and scientifically unsound philosophical speculation, which claims to have shattered the pre-eminent position of man within nature by discovering man's animal past. The true scientist experiences his exceptional position as *humanus* in his own field. It is the privilege of man alone to produce science, to investigate truth for the sake of truth, regardless of animal appetites and necessities.

If this is true, and the basis of humanism has not been shaken by modern science, it is all the more surprising that Copernicanism as well as Darwinism have actually produced effects within the course of spiritual history which point in the opposite direction. As a matter of fact, Copernicanism in the largest sense of the word, as well as Darwinism, *has* contributed to the dissolution of humanism and to the rise of present-day nihilism. Again, it is our task to try to understand this process and its causes in order to come to a true understanding of our present spiritual situation. It is to be expected that such an inquiry will produce important results. We ask first why Copernicanism has shaken the Christian Church and theology to such a degree that even in the beginning of the 18th century the government of the canton of Zürich strictly prohibited the discussion of this theory.[56] Looking back, the answer is not very difficult to find. Copernicanism had this effect because the Church did and had done for centuries what it should not have done. The Church had mixed up truth-of-God with world-truth. It had established and dogmatically canonised the Biblical world-picture of antiquity, which because of its origin we call the Babylonian world-picture, with its three stories: the flat plate of the earth; above it and on the same axis, so to speak, the sky or heaven; below it the underworld. This ancient world-picture is merely the vessel in which the divine revelation is given to man, but has itself nothing to do with that revelation. The Church and its theology therefore were forced by science to withdraw from a realm which was not theirs. Natural science has helped the Church to understand its own truth and essence better than it had understood them in the course of preceding centuries.

Nevertheless, Christian theology was not altogether wrong in its apprehension with regard to Copernicanism. Theology should not have opposed science, but it was right in opposing a certain philosophical consequence drawn from the Copernican discovery within the rationalistic humanism of the time. This Renaissance humanism in its turn used the new world-picture as a weapon against the Christian doctrine of revelation as such. It used the Copernican theory, as we see it, for instance, in the example of Giordano Bruno, as a foundation of Pantheistic philosophy and mysticism.[57] In the humanistic movement of emancipation from Christianity, Copernican astrophysics was quite unjustifiably impressed as an ally. Again, rational humanism is not alone to blame for having done this. It was the Church which, by her mistaken orthodoxy, had caused this error on the other side. The blow which the Church struck against Copernicus was warded off by rational humanism with a Copernican blow against the Church. However, whilst the Church recognised her error in course of time, the philosophy of Enlightenment, the heir and successor of Renaissance humanism, continued the fight on the same level, and does so to this day. In this manner Copernicanism became, although *per nefas,* an important element in the formation of a de-Christianised humanism.

The case of Darwinism is analogous. Once again Christian theology confused God-knowledge and world-knowledge, and fought fiercely against a strictly scientific hypothesis, *i.e.* the theory of evolution. In particular, it was Darwin's idea of man's animal origin which the Christian Church at first misconceived as a death-blow against a central Christian doctrine, namely man's being created in the image of God. This error was comprehensible and pardonable, because it took some hard thinking to disentangle the faith content of the *imago dei* doctrine from the traditional anthropological conceptions. But it was an error all the same.[58] This mistaken opposition to Darwinism on the part of Christian theology has, however, a positive side. It was not without reason that the Church was afraid of the false and most dangerous philosophical use that would be made of this scientific discovery—a use which, if it became victorious, would mean no less than the end of any kind of humanism. This erroneous and, in its consequences, fatally dangerous exploitation of Darwin's theory took place indeed in the development of an evolutionist system of philosophy in the latter part of the 19th century. The quintessence of this was the thesis that man is *nothing but* a highly differentiated animal. This "nothing but" theory was indeed the end of any kind of humanism and the beginning of the naturalistic nihilism of our day.

How was this evolutionist pseudo-scientific philosophy possible? It is necessary here to return to something which we have noted in a previous connection, namely to that transition from a truly idealist humanism grounded in an idealistic metaphysics to a positivistic anti-metaphysical philosophy. It is best understood if we take Kant as our starting point. From Kant's critical idealism, which gave rise to such genuine forms of humanism as that of Humboldt and Schiller, two very different philosophical schools developed: the absolute or speculative idealism of Fichte and Hegel on the one side, and an anti-metaphysical critical philosophy on the other, which led on to positivism. In Auguste Comte's *Religion de l'humanité* a remainder of ethical idealism survives, a reflection, so to speak, of idealistic light without a source of its own. The same is true in thinkers like John Stuart Mill and Herbert Spencer. They all hold a kind of ethical idealism cut off from its roots. All these philosophers eagerly and sincerely intend to salvage some kind of humanism, but cannot give it any satisfactory theoretical foundation. It was into this philosophical context that the Darwinist theory was launched, and by it developed into a system of evolutionism with the essential doctrine that man is *nothing but* a highly differentiated animal. It is obvious— although there are still many who do not know it—that on such a basis humanism of any kind is impossible. Humanism degenerates, if I may use the word, into a mere hominism.[59] The human becomes a mere natural datum. On such a naturalistic basis it is impossible to distinguish the human from the animal and to vindicate for man any kind of independence against nature. If the nature-continuum is the only reality, there can be no spiritual norms, no conscience, no higher destiny. The talk of "higher" and "lower" is then a mere *façon de parler;* it simply means biological differentiation which, as such, has nothing to do with value or norm. It is, then, easy to understand why, in the generation following Comte, Mill and Spencer, further development of the evolutionary system caused the last remainders of the idealistic humanism of earlier times to disappear. If man is nothing but the highly developed brain-species of the mammal-family, ideas such as man's dignity, personality, the rights of man, human destiny lose their meaning. The bankruptcy which, theoretically, already existed in the generation of Spencer was declared in the following decades; it only remained for the last generation to put it into execution.

The question arises: Was this inevitable and, if so, why? Our answer is that it was inevitable if the emancipation from Christian faith was to be carried through. We go back to the point at which the double process of dissociation set in, in the form of Reformation on the one hand, of Renaissance humanism on the other. The Reformation was a tremendous attempt to tear away from the traditional synthesis all those elements which were irreconcilable with a truly Biblical understanding of man and his destiny. That this attempt, grand as it was in its beginning, was not capable of working itself out on the scale which might have been expected, is primarily due to the fact that the genuine Christian element was covered and falsified by a false, orthodox absolutism, which necessarily provoked the reaction of rationalistic humanism. The philosophy of the Enlightenment is, in the first place, an unavoidable reaction against petrified Christian orthodoxy. But why did it come about that idealistic humanism degenerated more and more into positivist naturalistic "hominism"? I think the answer must be that the germ of degeneration lies in the very foundation of idealistic humanism itself, firstly, in its anthropology; secondly, in its metaphysics.

Idealism, in order to keep its conception of man, inevitably splits human personality into two parts: into an animal or sensual, and a spiritual or divine part. But what am I, this

VI]   IDEALISM AND INDIVIDUALITY   87

concrete individual man? If, according to the principle,
principium individuationis est materia, my individual personality belongs to the lower parts, then it has no spiritual foundation and dignity. If, however, personality belongs to the divine
part, how then could it be individual and plural? Idealism
separates spirit and nature. But am I the spirit, or is the spirit
my spirit? Since the days of the Stoics the attempt has been
made to solve this problem by the idea of a divine spark. Man's
mind is a spark of the divine spiritual fire. If that is so, its combination with an individual must be a kind of banishment, a
state of imprisonment, according to the old Pythagorean phrase :
σῶμα σῆμα (the body is a tomb). This individual spirit, then,
must tend to reintegration in the divine spirit, and individual
personality is merely a provisional, not an essential and definitive,
state of being. Then I, this individual personality, am destined
to perish, my higher part being consumed within the divine
spirit, my lower part going back to nature. Therefore it is not
I, this individual person, who stand over against the natural
world; but there are two general, impersonal entities opposite
one another, the universal divine mind or reason and material
nature. But I, this individual Ego, am destined to vanish into
these two universal impersonal entities. I, as personal individuality, am not superior to nature, my individual self is lost either
way. What does it matter whether it is lost in the divine mind
or in material nature? It is this doubt of the value of individual
personality which is inherent in all idealism, and this is one of
the sources of the further degeneration. What interest can
individual man have in a kind of humanism which is so dis-
interested in the metaphysical value of individual personality?

The second point is closely related to the first. Ancient
humanism grew out of ancient religion; its metaphysics was a
rational transformation of pre-Christian religion and mythology.
Now this religion was destroyed by Christianity and no enthusiasm for classical Greece could revive it. Modern idealistic
humanism grew out of the Christian tradition. It was, so to
speak, a rational by-product of Christian theology. In so far as
this humanism, following its tendency to rationality, detached

itself from its Christian foundation, its metaphysical content became thin and uncertain. True, there were some powerful thinkers who were able to develop an idealistic metaphysic as the foundation of this humanism. But these systems were, first, altogether comprehensible only to a small elite of qualified thinkers and could not affect the large majority. Apart from this, such a theoretical idealism was too abstract, not to say abstruse, to be a plausible solution of the problem of reality. Already in the first half of the 19th century this idealism had played out its rôle. It was, as we have already seen, only the non-metaphysical idealism which remained, and which formed also the transition to that positivist philosophy which was the grave of all true humanism. An idealism which was only capable of holding fast ideal values and postulates, without any foundation in being, had no power of resistance against the wave of naturalist realism with its causal explanation of everything, including man. Thus the emancipation from Christianity, which in the time of the Renaissance was begun with so much enthusiasm, ended in a stark, crude naturalism within which there was no room for genuine human values.

True *Christian* humanism is, however, still an unfinished project in a world hitherto called Christian. It is a debt which the Christian Church owes to the world to this day. Christianity cannot be exculpated from a great share of guilt in the modern attempt to found a rational humanism independent of Church dogma and Church authority. This is not the time, however, to portion out the guilt of the past, but to find the basis of a true humanism. It is the task of the lectures which follow to show why this basis can be found only in Biblical revelation. In this lecture we have been dealing with one aspect of the problem only: man's place in the Universe.

The Christian doctrine of man's being created in the image of God does two things: it places man within nature and at the same time elevates him above it. Like all nature, man in his totality is a creature. Just as that psalmist, who had to teach us such important things about the true perspective of the world, was able to reconcile both his being created by God and his

origin as an embryo in his mother's womb,[60] so the truly
Christian conception of man does not reject the idea that the
human race has its origins in a pre-human realm.　And just as
the men speaking to us in the Bible always knew that man is as
nothing in the God-created Universe, a truly Christian conception of man does not exclude the idea that in the spatial Universe
there is no above and no below and no middle.　At the same
time, the Christian knows that God has called him to the
dominion over all the earth, because He has created man, and
man alone, in such a way that he has to execute God's will, not in
blind, dumb and ignorant necessity, but in hearing God's word
and answering Him by his own decision.　In this call he re-
cognises the deepest foundation of his personal being and his
elevation over all the rest of creation.　It is through this God-
given dominion over nature that he is given the power and the
right not merely to use natural forces, but also to investigate
nature by his own God-given reason.　But the man who knows
himself as bound by the word of the Creator, and responsible to
Him, will not misuse his scientific knowledge of the world by
using his reason to raise himself up against the Creator and to
emancipate himself from Him by a false pretence of autonomy.
He will not become one who, detached from God, is the prisoner
of his own technical achievements.　Of that we shall speak
later on.

This doctrine of the *imago dei* does not, however, stand on its
own right, but is comprehensible in its deepest meaning only
from the centre of divine self-revelation.　Behind Christian
humanism stands, as its basic foundation, the faith in that Man
in whom both the mystery of God and the secret of man have
been revealed in one; the belief that the Creator of the Universe
attaches Himself to man; that He, in whose creative word the
whole structure of the Universe has its foundation, has made
known as His world purpose the restoration and perfection of
His image in man; that therefore not only the history of humanity, but the history of the whole Cosmos shall be consummated in
God-humanity.　It is this aspect of the Christian conception of
man that gives him his incomparable and unique place in the
Universe.

Nothing that astro-physical science has brought or will bring to light about the structure of this Universe, and nothing that biological science has discovered or will discover about the connection between sub-human and human organisms, can shake or even touch this truly Christian theanthropocentricism.   If it is true that God created man in His image, and that this image is realised in Christ's God-manhood—and faith knows this to be true—then nothing, either in the sphere of nature or in that of history, can uproot this humanism, unless it be the loss of this faith.   But where this faith is kept, where it is alive in the power and purity of its origin in the revelation of the New Testament, there Christian humanism does not merely consist of a humanistic conception of man and his place in the Universe, but is at the same time a power which must stamp all aspects of daily life as well as cultural life at large with the mark of true humanity.

VII

PERSONALITY AND HUMANITY

THE history of mankind begins with collectivism. Primitive man and primitive society do not know individual personality. Man is an entirely generic being. The individual does what everyone does, thinks what people as a whole think. Just as primitive man does not clearly distinguish himself from the animal, so the individual is not distinct within the collectivity. The collective mind completely dominates primitive society. The oldest civilisations which we know, those of Egypt and Babylon, are thoroughly collectivist. Their cultural achievements remain anonymous with the one exception of the king. But his elevation from the anonymous remainder is not due to his personality, but to his social-political function. It is exactly this fact—that the king, as bearer of highest public authority, bears divine attributes and is revered as a being descending from the gods—which shows the tremendous predominance of the collectivist and institutional over the personal.

In the discovery of individual personality Greece is the pioneer nation. Perhaps we might claim the myth of Prometheus as the earliest beginning of the emancipation of the individual. No doubt in this process the tragedy of Aeschylus, Sophocles and Euripides plays an important part. But even before that there began, not in Athens but in Asia Minor, a detachment of the individual from collectivity and its institutions. This is the significance of philosophical reflection as it originated on the shores of Asia Minor and in Sicily and which significantly developed from the start as a rival to myth. Now, for the first time, there are some bold individuals who dare to think independently, to criticise mythology and to emancipate themselves from tradition. In Athens the democratic republic is founded as an expression of the same mind; sophistic philosophy and individualising comedy, with its acid criticism of society, arise simultaneously. Single creative individualities come to the fore; works of culture are called after their creators; individual fame is no longer limited to military bravery, that is, to action in favour of collective security, but passes over to thinkers, poets, artists. Fame is not only, as we are apt to think nowadays, a matter of personal vanity and ambition; the phenomenon of fame shows that the individual becomes conscious of his personal value. It is by this process that classical antiquity becomes a model which has never been surpassed for individualised cultural activity and individualised humanity. The human face presents itself in an innumerable plurality of markedly individual faces.

Moreover, it is as if this emancipation from collectivity had no sooner begun than it ran to the opposite extreme. In sophistic philosophy, individualism has already reached such a radical expression of extreme subjectivism that Athenian society is shaken to its moral and religious foundations. It is about the same time that Athenian democracy is in danger of falling prey to an anarchic mob-rule. The emancipation of the individual seems to end in a complete, sceptical dissolution of all objective norms. But, thanks to unspent moral and religious reserves, to a prevailing sense of social necessity, and—last but not least— thanks to the great achievement of Platonic and Aristotelian philosophy, this subjectivist sophism remained an episode or a crisis which was overcome. It is only after this that Greek humanism reasserts itself, and the concept of humanity and the human is formed.[61]

In the full sense this is not yet true of Plato and Aristotle, because for them the humane is identical with the Hellenic. Beyond the realm of the Greek language begins that of the barbarians, which cannot be considered as truly human. And for those great thinkers the existence of the slave—that is, the man without dignity or rights—is taken for granted. But this limitation of classical philosophy is soon overcome in Hellenistic, particularly Stoic, philosophy. The vision extends itself beyond the Greek into the human as such; the sense of humanity as a whole is formed for the first time; the word *homo sum* becomes the highest title of nobility. The recognition of the indestructible human dignity of every being having a human face becomes the highest ethical principle. The principle of humanity is discovered and is, one must say, preached—not only taught—with a high religious feeling, particularly by the later Stoics on Roman soil. So it might appear that classical antiquity, the Greek mind, has done all that was to be done in the discovery of humanity. It has brought forth both individual personality and universal humanity.

All the same, it was not this Greek humanism which became the main foundation of Western humanism. That was kept in store for another power of a totally different character—for Christianity. No doubt the Christian Church has absorbed within itself since the time of the earliest Fathers a good portion of the ancient classical heritage of civilisation and humanism, but the fundamental conception of man's essence and of true humanity was a totally different one, not only in its basis, but also in its content and in its practical consequences.

I should like to formulate this fundamental difference between the Christian and the Greek conception of humanity in three points: in the idea of personality, in that of community, and in the relation between body and spirit. It will appear that those three points are in close necessary relation, so that we might call them rather three aspects of one and the same thing.

1. We have been trying to show how much the Greek mind has done for the discovery and appreciation of individual personality. But the Greek idea of man is threatened by a fatal either/or, which can be seen by a comparative study of the older Platonic-Aristotelian and the later Stoic concepts of the human. In Plato and Aristotle a certain appreciation of individual personality becomes possible by envisaging the articulation of reason, proportional to its different functions. The consequence of this individualising view is a scale or hierarchy of different groups like the Greeks and the barbarians, the men and the women, the free and the slaves. In Plato's state we are faced

with a real caste-system based on this idea.[62] Now the Stoics dropped this hierarchical conception, and by that gave the principle of humanity its full universality. Every man is essentially equal to every other man, because the same divine reason is indwelling in every one. But whilst this idea is the cause of the universality of humanity, it also produces the impersonal, abstract concept of man which strikes us in Stoic writings. It is not this man here, in his individual being, who is the object of my appreciation, but it is the divine reason dwelling in him, dwelling in all identically. It is therefore an abstract, impersonal, general principle to which our evaluation is directed and which makes man human.[63]

The Christian concept of personality is entirely different. Here it is the call of God, summoning me, this individual man, to communion with Him, which makes me a person, a responsible being. "I have called Thee by Thy name, Thou art mine." A divine *I* calls me *Thou* and attests to me that I, this individual man, being here and being so, am seen and called by God from eternity. This dignity of human personality is not grounded in an abstract, general element in all men, namely reason, but individual personality as such is the object of this appreciation because it is deemed worthy of being called by God. Only the personal God can fundamentally establish truly personal existence and responsibility, responsibility being the inescapable necessity to answer God's creative call, and to answer it so that this answer is also a decision. God's call in love shall be answered by man's response in love. By doing this—by loving God as he is loved by God—man is similar to God. The loving man, having received God's love, is God's image. The love of the personal God does not create an abstract, impersonal humanity; it calls the individual to the most personal responsibility.

2. With this first element, the second is in the closest connection, namely the relation to community. As in Greek philosophy reason is the *principium humanitatis,* no relation to communion is based on it. Abstract reason does not tend to communion, but to unity. In thinking I am related to general truth, to ideas, not to the Thou of my neighbour. Activity of

reason has its meaning in itself, the wise man is self-sufficient, he has no desire to go out from himself to another. In Christian faith, however, it is the same thing that makes me an individual person, which also leads me necessarily to my fellow-man: the love of God. God in His free grace gives man His love and calls him to receive it in order to give it back. Not reason, but love is the *principium humanitatis*. In such a way, this love, given on the part of God, determines both the relation to God and the relation to the fellow-man. "Thou shalt love the Lord thy God," and the command that follows is equal with it: "Thou shalt love thy neighbour as thyself." More than that, it is not the divine commandment but the divine gift of love which is the basis of true personality. God gives man His own love, but He gives it in such a way that it cannot be received save in a free act of reception, in responsive love, which is faith. Greek idealism is a system of *unity;* Christianity, however, is revealed communion.

This means the creation of a humanism of a very different character from that of Greek idealism. Not reason, but love is the truly human. Reason, spiritual activity, is subordinate to love. It is an instrument of love. This is to say, also, that civilisation is not in itself the essentially human, but is, in its turn, an instrument, an expression, not in itself a purpose. In the same way the rational principle of *autarkia,* self-sufficiency, characteristic of the wise philosopher, is here impossible. Man cannot become truly human except by entering into community. He is called by the loving God into a loving relation to his fellow-man.

3. This opposition in the basis of the idea of humanity—immanent divine reason in the one hand, the transcendent divine call of love on the other—expresses itself in a third sense in a most characteristic and momentous manner. The Greek principle of reason brings with it a dualistic conception of man. Man is composed of two parts. By his reason, that is his higher element, he shares in the divine being; by his body, that is his lower element, man partakes of animal nature, out of which comes evil. The one is the basis of his dignity; the other is the

cause of his ignominy, which can be mitigated only by the fact
that this lower part may be called unessential or accidental.
The Christian faith, answering the call of love of the Creator,
produces quite a different view of man's structure.   The whole
man, body and mind, is God's creation.   There is no more
reason to despise the body than there is to consider human
rationality as divine.   The whole man, body and mind, is called
into communion with God and into the service of God.   Therefore there is no question here of the ascetic ideal, inherent in
idealism since Plato's *Phaedo*, that the spiritual is to be delivered
out of its entanglement with the body, or that this spiritual
freedom is to be maintained over against the world outside.
Here the task is to co-operate in the totality of this corporal-
spiritual personality with the work of God in the world, to give
oneself in love into this service, which is at the same time a
service for God and for man, and which is the expression of the
freedom and nobility of the children of God.   We can guess
even now what a different conception of manual work must
result from these two different anthropologies.   The ascetic
spiritualism, however, as we find it in the mediæval Church, is
not of Christian but of Hellenistic origin, and is an exact
parallel to the Neoplatonic element in mediæval philosophy.

Now, taking these elements in their unity—the principle of
immanence on the one hand, the divine relation of love and
reciprocal service on the other—a further essential difference is
revealed.   In one of the most beautiful passages of Aristotle's
Nicomachæan ethics, the chapter on friendship,[64] the great
thinker pronounces as a matter of course that one can love only
those who are worthy of being loved. To love someone unworthy
would be a sign of an ignoble mind, a sign of a lack of the sense
of value.   Now, Christian love is founded in God's love for
sinful and unworthy man.   This love, then, is received in the
consciousness of being unworthy of it; that means that underlying the Christian *humanitas* we find *humilitas*.   Humility
is the most unambiguous sign of true love, just as love for the
unworthy is its most genuine expression.   This is the trait which
distinguishes Christian humanity most markedly from the

idealistic Greek, and which is also the great scandal for many humanists. It is, at bottom, the scandal and foolishness of the Cross which become apparent here.

During the first fifteen centuries of the Christian era these two forms of humanism—the Christian and the idealistic Greek—lived together in a kind of association or amalgam without any awareness of the specific character of either of them. Then, in the middle of the second millenium, that double-sided process of dissociation took place, of which we were speaking in the last lecture, and which is the essence of the two principal movements, the Renaissance and the Reformation. In the course of the following centuries it became apparent that the temper of the modern age favoured the first of these two movements. Mankind was out to find an immanent and rational basis of civilisation, and therefore gave preference to the Renaissance conception of humanism. This, however, meant a progressive detachment of European civilisation from its previously Christian basis. The phases of this movement have already been sketched. The starting point is a theism still closely connected with the Christian; it is therefore a humanism based on a religious-metaphysical foundation, whilst the terminus of this movement is a naturalist positivism, which is not capable of giving a basis to any kind of humanism, whether Christian or Greek. The question consequently arises as to why the original programme of Renaissance humanism, *i.e.* the restoration of the Greek idea of humanity, was not carried out; or, to put it better, why the process of emancipation from Christianity was not successfully arrested in a revived classical humanism.

The answer to this question comes from what was said in the last lecture. Greek humanism had not been a *creatio ex nihilo*. It had been the rational transformation of ancient pagan religion and drew much of its power of conviction from this religious-metaphysical presupposition. Now this presupposition could not be reproduced, pre-Christian religion having been completely destroyed by Christianity. The humanism of the Renaissance and even of the beginning of the Enlightenment could remain unconscious of this fact as long as it still drew its life from the

metaphysical substance of the *Christian* tradition. But in so far
as this connection was lost, or consciously cut, the idealistic
humanism was hanging in the air. The systems of philosophical
metaphysics could not be an equivalent substitute for the lost
religious basis, if only for the reason that they were accessible
only to a small elite of philosophical thinkers. This metaphysical background was definitely and purposely pushed aside
by the positivist movement and from that moment humanism had lost its basis. More and more it was replaced by a
naturalistic inhumanism, by a materialist collectivism, by a
pseudo-Darwinian principle of ruthless extinction of the weaker
by the stronger, or by a pseudo-romantic principle of the
powerful individual dominating the mass of the herd-people.

I should like to illustrate this general movement more con-
cretely by showing the effect of this process within those same
three spheres in which we have just been defining the difference
between Greek and Christian humanism. The first of these
points was the Christian foundation of personality in divine
election, in the personal call of the personal God. Now, for this
transcendent basis of personality was first substituted the
immanent principle of divine reason. In the beginning of
rational humanism—for instance that of Erasmus or that of
John Locke—this divine reason still had a close kinship with the
Christian idea of God. These fathers of rational humanism
were not even conscious of breaking away from Christian revelation, but believed themselves to be within the Biblical tradition.
But the rupture, which had taken place unconsciously, became
increasingly apparent. The principle of reason was more and
more divested of its transcendent content. The metaphysical
interpretation, as it was given in the systems of idealistic philosophy, could not resist the stream of modern secularism.

We can observe this change from a half-transcendental to a
flatly secularist interpretation of human nature in the development of the three most important pupils of Hegel, namely
Feuerbach, Strauss and Marx. Whilst they all started as ardent
followers of Hegel's absolute idealism, they all ended in a flat
naturalism of a more or less materialistic character. But all of

them tried to retain some humanistic elements, although without any theoretical justification. Feuerbach tries to safeguard some elements of the idea of personality in his conception of the individual,[65] whilst Marx sacrifices personality to the system—not to a system of ideas in the fashion of Hegel, but to the realistic system of economy, in which the individual plays a very subordinate rôle. Strauss, in his turn, comes out with a blunt materialism softened only with a light aesthetic colouring, which was all that remained of idealistic humanism. It was this poor figure which provoked the wrath of another champion of the new type of anthropology, Friedrich Nietzsche. His programme is the total " transvaluation of values ", by declaring war on all " backworlders ", as he calls the adherents of any kind of religion or metaphysics, and the proclamation of the powerful individual rising above the average mass and using it as the material of his will to power. Behind these conceptions of Marx and Nietzsche we see already dawning upon mankind the monstrous figure of the totalitarian state, either in its post-Marxian Communist or in its post-Nietzschean Fascist form—that totalitarian state in which human personality is practically denied and abolished.

It would, however, be erroneous to think that this degeneration of humanism had taken place only within the spiritual history of Germany. Contemporaneously with that materialistic development of Hegelianism, there arises in France Auguste Comte's " philosophie positive ", with its negation of all metaphysics and its proclamation of a *Religion de l'humanité*. In England there was a similar school of thought, led by men like Stuart Mill and Herbert Spencer, with a similar tendency to interpret man from merely immanent presuppositions, and still to try to keep some humanistic elements within a naturalistic context which was incapable of affording a basis for them. The idea of evolution, forming the backbone in the French as well as in the English system of positivist philosophy, was incapable of safeguarding anything like an idea of personality, either in the Greek or in the Christian meaning of the word. A highly differentiated animal is no personality, personality being—in distinction from a differentiated brain-animal—a certain relation to transcendent truth, be it (as in the Greek conception) the relation to the divine Logos, or (as in the Christian conception) the relation to the person of the Creator. All the readiness of individual positivists to retain the moral values of the Greek-Christian tradition was in vain. You cannot have apples after having chopped down all the apple-trees. That is why in the following decades the representatives of this positivist, naturalistic philosophy had to accept the consequences. They threw out of their vocabulary the idea of human dignity and human rights and substituted for them more realistic terms which fitted into their naturalistic system.[66] It is, humanly speaking, almost by chance that the domination of this philosophy in other countries did not produce there the same effect that it did in Germany and Russia, namely the totalitarian state, which is nothing but positivist philosophy put into practice.

The change from idealism to naturalistic positivism becomes particularly intelligible if we view it from the second stand-point, the problem of community. Those early humanists of the Renaissance and Enlightenment, who consciously or unconsciously tried to emancipate humanism from its Christian basis, were certainly not conscious of the fact that they thereby created a sociological alternative of the gravest consequences. In the Christian faith these two things are simultaneously and equally granted: the independent standing of personality and the necessity of community. It is the same call of God which summons the individual to his freedom and independent dignity and which summons him into communion and mutual responsibility. The unity of personality and community is rooted in the Christian God-idea alone. Apart from this basis the two cannot co-exist. Apart from the Christian foundation this unity breaks up into an either/or of individualist liberalism and collectivist authoritarianism.

Idealistic humanism in itself has always been an aristocratic doctrine. It is the life-conception of a bourgeois few. The immanent divine reason, being the basis of personality, creates the *autarky* of individual personality, the Stoic sage, who has no need of anyone else. The humanist of the idealistic type is a spiritual aristocrat, knowing that he has the divine spark in himself and is therefore essentially independent. What leads him to community is nothing essential, but merely outward necessity, and this community is in itself not real communion but a combination of a contractual character. There is no original, organically necessary community, but only that kind of community which comes about through certain purposes and is therefore regulated by some kind of *contrat social*. It is not the State only, but also marriage and every kind of community, which rests on some kind of *contrat social*. Why should one enter into a fundamental interdependence if every individual has the essential in himself? Within this context community can never be on the same level as independent personality, but only something subordinate and casual. That is to say that idealistic humanism leads to an individualistic conception of society, which in the end must have anarchical consequences. That is why modern society, in so far as it has relinquished its Christian basis, appears to be in a state of latent anarchy or dissolution.

With the middle of the 19th century there begins a fierce reaction against this individualism, and this collectivist reaction in its turn is worked out logically from a naturalist philosophy. The alternative to idealistic individualism is not free communion, but primitive tribal, not to say animal, collectivism. It is the depersonalised mass-man, the man forming a mere particle of a social structure and the centralised, automatic, mechanical totalitarian state, which inherits the decaying liberal democracy. Only where a strong Christian tradition had prevailed was it possible to avoid this fatal alternative of individualism and collectivism, to preserve a federal, non-centralised, pluralistic, organic structure of the State, and therefore to avoid that sudden transition from a half anarchic individualism into a tyrannical totalitarianism. But the societies of the West, which abhor the way taken by totalitarian Russia, Italy and Germany, do not yet seem to have grasped that, if the process of de-Christianisation goes on within their society, they, too, will inevitably go the same way.

The third point—namely the relation between spirit and

nature—remains to be taken into consideration in order to see these things clearly. In Christian faith man is seen as a spiritual-corporeal unity; God is the creator not only of man's spirit, but also of his body. Therefore the bodily life has its own dignity in the sight of God, and man is called into the service of bodily needs as into a sacred service. The body is " the temple of the Holy Spirit ".[67] In the Christian Sacrament an indissoluble connection of material bread and spiritual eating is expressed. In the middle of the Lord's Prayer stands the petition for daily bread. All this works together to make impossible a one-sided spirituality. Man need not be ashamed of his body and his bodily needs.

For idealist humanism, on the other hand, this bodily constitution of man—this animal part, as he calls it—is the *partie honteuse* of his existence, his dignity resting entirely on his spirit, which is his divine part. It is the animal impulse of the body from which moral evil originates. It is the sensible impressions and perceptions which keep the mind from forming truly spiritual conceptions. The whole humanistic system of values is based upon this contrast or opposition of animal nature and divine spirit. It is therefore the liberation of the spirit from the body which is the guiding idea of humanistic culture.[68] It is obvious that such a humanism cannot have much interest in the economic conditions of man's life. That man is a being who must eat, who has hunger, is a topic which remains outside this dignified culture. There is no Holy Supper here, nor is there a prayer for the daily bread to remind the spiritual humanist of the sacredness of the body.

So exalted a spirituality could never be the spiritual home of the average man. Much less could it be so, when—through the Industrial Revolution—the economic element became the dominating feature of his life. In the middle of the 19th century this aristocratic spirituality had become impossible. The reaction against this spirituality was inevitable. And come it did, primarily in the form of a doctrine which placed the economic element in the very centre of the whole of human life, making it the very essence of human history, as did the historical materialism of Karl Marx. The change could not be more dramatic. Marx, the pupil of the philosopher who had proclaimed the spirit as the only reality, became the creator of a theory in which ideas and spiritual values were but an *Ueberbau*, a superstructure, an appendix or reflex of economic processes. But Marx is not the only one to make such a sudden *volte-face.* There was also Friedrich Nietzsche, a solitary thinker and poet, who came from a most dignified tradition of humanism and scholarship, and yet proclaimed with prophetic vehemence that doctrine of the transvaluation of all values, which means the primacy of instinct above the spirit and the will to power as the new principle of ethics. Aristocrat and individualist through and through, he could not prevent his teaching from becoming the programme of a mass movement, comparable in size and vehemence only to the one which Karl Marx had produced. Was it to be wondered at that the masses getting hold of this programme took literally Nietzsche's prophecy of the emancipation of instinct from the fetters of metaphysics and religion, and understood his doctrine of the will to power to mean what it said, namely that it was a practical application of the Darwinian principle of the struggle for life in which the strong survive at the cost of the weak?

Marx and Nietzsche[69] are the fathers of the totalitarian revolutions and of totalitarian states. It seems paradoxical that the extremest collectivism and the extremest individualism should flow together in one stream. But upon closer inspection this fact is not at all paradoxical. The common denominator of both systems is the complete depersonalisation of man. Whether you understand man primarily as the animal, that has hunger, or by the two categories of the herd-animals and the solitary beasts of prey terrorising the herds, you come to the same result, namely the elimination of man's personality, human dignity, and the rights of man, placing them all on the level of nature-phenomena. Naturalistic philosophy, whether of the Marxist rationalist or of the Nietzschean romantic type, necessarily means depersonalisation. In Communist totalitarianism, on the one hand, and in National-Socialist totalitarianism on the other, the seed of Karl Marx and Friedrich Nietzsche has germinated, and in these two monstrosities, which are one in essence, the movement of emancipation from Christianity has reached its goal. This goal is, in both cases, the annihilation of the truly human, the end of humanism.

We should not close this survey without one further observation. Why did that whole movement of emancipation arise? Is it *entirely* due to man's unwillingness to bow his head before the divine revelation, because he wants to hold his head high as his own lord? Is the modern movement away from Christianity exclusively caused by the desire for an autonomous reason? Is not a cause also to be found within the presentation of this Christian revelation by empirical Christianity? In other words, should not the Christian Church take on its own shoulders a part of the burden of responsibility for this tragic history? If we think of that third point about which we have just been speaking—the false separation of body and spirit, of bread and divine will—we cannot ignore the fact that empirical Christianity has been untrue to its own truth. The Christians of almost all centuries have been guilty of a one-sided, false spiritualism which neglected the daily bread for the spiritual bread and by a false monastic or puritan disparagement of the body and its impulses brought about the revolt of an ill-treated human nature. The same could be said with regard to the other two points. If the modern age is characterised by a false secularism or this-worldliness, traditional Christianity certainly has to accept the verdict of a false other-worldliness which, in its interest in the eternal life, forgot the task of this earthly life. And finally, whilst it is true that the unity of the truly personal and the truly communal is grounded in the Christian revelation taken in its original truth, empirical Christianity has failed to a large extent to prove this unity practically. On the one hand, it has produced an authoritarian, pseudo-sacred collectivism, a Church of power and spiritual slavery; on the other hand, it has produced an orthodox misunderstanding of faith, *i.e.* a kind of faith which was not united with love but was morally sterile, and which therefore could not but repel those who had grasped something of the gospel of love.   It is a provable fact that these short-comings of Christianity were among the main impulses of the humanistic emancipation-movement.   Thus, the de-Christianisation characteristic of the modern age is, to a large extent, the product of the infidelity of the Christians to their own faith.[70]

Christian faith itself, understood in its purity, is the only sure basis for, and an inexhaustible fountain of, a true humanism. But it is no exception to that rule: *corruptio optimi pessima*. The history of empirical Christianity is unhappily not only a testimony of truest, and purest, and sublimest humanity, but also in many cases it affords the sad spectacle of incredible in-humanity.   Therefore the Gospel of Jesus Christ is not only a judgment upon the secularised godless, but also upon the godlessness of the Church and of the pious, who so often forgot that faith in the Crucified implies the willingness to sacrifice, and that the ultimate criterion of faith is faithfulness in the service of the fellow-man.

But, whilst all this is true with regard to empirical Christen-dom taken as a whole, it does not touch the Christian Gospel as such.   All these short-comings are due to a misunderstanding of God's revelation in Christ and to the failure of the Christian Church to be truly Christian.   It does not disprove in the least that the Gospel of God's love is the only solid basis of a true humanism which safeguards the dignity of individual person-ality, essential, non-accidental community, and the unity of mankind.

VIII

THE PROBLEM OF JUSTICE [71]

IT is one of the paradoxes of modern history that in hardly
any previous epoch has there been so much discussion of,
and so vehement demand for justice as in ours; and that at
the same time it is precisely those movements to which this
demand for justice has given rise which have led us into a
condition that seems to be further off from justice than any
other. The idea of justice, although at first sight apparently a
rational and timeless element, is historical and variable. In this
sphere, as in most others, there are historical heritages that can
be acquired and lost again. No doubt there is a sense or feeling
of justice in every human being. It expresses itself in the most
unambiguous and spontaneous manner, particularly where one's
own right has been violated by others. But the contents which
kindle this feeling, the concrete notions of what is just and
unjust, are different in different times and within the different
civilisations.

In the first place we have to point to the connection between
justice and religious or metaphysical ideas. Whilst the occasion
on which, in the beginnings of history, the problem of justice
became acute was a thoroughly secular one, namely the judgment of the judge, yet the idea or the feeling that this, the
pronouncement of judgment, is a holy affair is hardly lacking
anywhere. It is obvious that in all ancient civilisations the judge
is a sacred personality, standing under divine protection and
acting under the authority of a divine mandate. Whereas the
foreground of the judgment-court is a civic, secular institution,
its background is, more or less symbolically, visible divinity.
There is a divine order to which the action of the judge refers.
The civic order must somehow copy the divine order; the human
sentence must correspond to a divine will. This relation becomes

particularly apparent where the sentence of the judge is not merely the application of a written law, but a free finding. In this case the request for just judgment directly implies that relation to the superhuman order in which the just is presupposed: to listen to this transcendent voice and to obey its intimations is exactly what is meant by the objectivity and justice of the judge's sentence.

Such a metaphysical or religious relation is included in the idea of justice which for many centuries has been predominant in the Western world. It is the idea of *jus naturale* or *lex naturae*, in which the two main lines of our cultural tradition, the Christian and the Greek heritage, are combined in a synthesis of exceptional power. For more than two thousand years the idea of *lex naturae* or *jus naturale* has been the basic conception within the European understanding of justice, and one of the pillars of European civilisation. Its origin is pre-Socratic Greece. Solon, the great law-giver of Athens, pronounced it as the norm of his legislative activity. To him as well as to his successors the idea of the φύσει δίκαιον, translated by the Roman Stoics into *lex naturae*, was intimately and inseparably connected with the idea of *divine* justice. That which is φύσει δίκαιον is the opposite of all human arbitrariness as well as of mere opportunism. The φύσει δίκαιον, the *lex naturae*, carries with it a deeply religious emotional content, from which the ethical demand for rigid objectivity is derived. Justice is something holy; is it backed by divine order, divine necessity.

It was this religious basis of *lex naturae*, of the " natural law ", that made it possible for Christian thinkers of early times to incorporate this central idea of ancient civilisation into the Christian system of thought. What the Greeks called " nature ", and what to them was the unity of divine and natural order, had to be interpreted in Christian terms as the order of the Creator or the order of creation. In creating the world, God has given to all things their order and by that their law. So, and not otherwise, the Creator wanted them to be. It is only within the last two or three decades that this idea of the divine order of creation, or *lex naturae*, has been suspected of being a form of natural theology which could not be acknowledged within a truly Christian conception of God, man and world. But the idea of *lex naturae*, or orders of creation, in no way prejudices the question of natural theology. When the Church Fathers were speaking of *lex naturae*, they connected it with that Logos in whom the whole world is created and in whom creation has its order, that Logos who became flesh in Jesus Christ. The Son of God, incarnate in Christ, is the principle of the divine order of creation and therefore of *lex naturae*. That is to say, the Christian Church never had a *lex naturae* conception other than a Christological one. *Lex naturae* was referred to that Creator of nature who revealed Himself in Christ Jesus.[72]

It must be admitted, however, that a certain relation to natural theology does exist in so far as these orders of creation and the principle of justice grounded in them, as well as the moral law, are not entirely unknown to natural man. Whilst the pagans do not know the Creator—or do not know Him properly, as He can be known by His revelation in Christ—they still know something of His orders, of His law. That is why they know something of justice, although the depth of Christian justice remains hidden from them. Justice, then, is a topic where Christian and non-Christian thinking meet, where they have a common ground without being identical. For this reason alone it is possible to have a civil order, the justice of which can be judged by Christian as well as non-Christian citizens, and an international order agreed upon by Christian as well as non-Christian nations. This was the reason why the theologians of the first centuries were able to accept the Stoic idea of *lex naturae* without hesitation, and to incorporate it into Christian theology and juridical vocabulary. They could not do it, however, without giving it a new interpretation. They had to take it out of its Pantheistic context and place it within the theological structure of Biblical revelation. They applied to it the principle that the book of divine creation could be read truly only in the light of historical revelation. Before we enter this problem of the specifically Christian interpretation of justice, I should like to follow the history of this idea to its end.

This history, broadly speaking, runs parallel to that of humanism, which we tried to sketch in previous lectures. It is an almost ludicrous misunderstanding, widespread as it is among the jurists on the Continent, that Hugo Grotius is the creator of natural law. The truth is that with Hugo Grotius begins the decay of natural law, which had been the ruling concept for two thousand years. For it was Grotius who for the first time tried to detach natural law from its religious, metaphysical basis. It was his explicit opinion that natural law would be valid even if there were no God, because it was rooted in reason. Now, Grotius certainly was a great scholar, but not so great a thinker; for otherwise he could not have failed to become aware of the contradiction which existed between his Christian idea of God and this idea of a reason and justice independent of God. But Grotius stands in the beginning of this movement, the main tendency of which is to detach the idea of justice entirely from its theological or religious or metaphysical context. The history of this movement is marked by the same milestones as that of humanism: a religious foundation of the idea of justice, without being Christian; a transcendental foundation, without being religious; assertion of the idea of justice as such on purely naturalistic grounds; and, finally, the reinterpretation of justice as a merely fictitious idea forming an instrument of self-preservation. In that manner the idea of justice is dissolved and the end is an ethical nihilism proclaiming the will to power or the autonomy of the economic motive. " If the salt has lost its savour, wherewith shall it be salted? " If the idea of justice is nothing but a conventional fiction, it has lost its normative power. It may then be that justice is nothing but camouflage for power interests, and that is its end.[73]

Thus it is not surprising that a totalitarian state draws the practical consequences of this result of the development of ideas. The totalitarian state exists ideally in the moment when the *jus divinum* is abolished, when the state is sovereign in the sense of not being limited by any higher power, when it can declare whatever it likes to be law, when there are no rights of man which precede positive law and are valid whether positive law proclaims them or not. The totalitarian state is the practical consequence of the positivist philosophy of law. The positivist conception of law has done away, theoretically, with the idea of justice, the totalitarian state does so practically in ridiculing the *jus divinum* and abolishing the rights of man.

The Western world, being surprised and shocked by the rise of totalitarianism, has, however, little justification for complaining or passing judgment on this latest phase of our modern history, because for many generations it has helped to prepare it. It has done so in a double fashion. First, as we have just seen, by a gradual process of detaching the conception of justice from its religious basis it has made justice a mere conventional fiction of society and politics. This positivist conception of justice— this negation of the *jus divinum*—was certainly not a speciality of those countries which later on became totalitarian.[74] England, as well as France and Switzerland, has played its part in this fatal European development of ideas. It was not seen that, if there is no *jus divinum*, there is no *limit* to the sovereignty of the state, there are no rights which the state has to *protect*, but only rights which the state may *give or take*. It was through the general blindness of the positivist era that the treasures of the Christian tradition, immanent in our social structure, were lost. It is this positivist philosophy which has prepared the totalitarian state. By the same token, it is the totalitarian state, carrying the positivist philosophy to its conclusion, which makes us see again the true nature of this positivist philosophy on the one hand, and the religious implication of the idea of justice on the other.

The second factor responsible for recent developments is not so much of a direct as of an indirect nature. The rationalistic form of natural law, as it was worked out during the 17th and 18th centuries—that form of natural law which seems to be almost the only one known to the average jurist—is characterised by a one-sided identification of justice and equality. According to this, justice is equality. The idea of equality was the dynamic element within newer political and social history. The idea of equality was the lever by which the *ancien régime*, the feudal

structure of society which had been based on inequality, was
thrown off its hinges. Equality was the great word of the French
Revolution. It was with his *Treatise on the Inequality of Man*
that Rousseau began his revolutionary critique of society.
It is the idea of equality on which modern democracy, following
Rousseau, is built. Equality is the by-name as well as the
ethical element in the newer Communist-Socialist movement,
in the political emancipation of woman, and in the social emancipation of youth. Equality in the name of justice! It is
because equality and justice are identified that—as we said in the
beginning—there has been so much more talk about justice in
our time than in any other. What was meant was always
equality.

Now it cannot be denied that there exists a close relation
between justice and equality, and that therefore the request for
equality partakes to a high degree in that profound, deeply
ethical and religious justification which is necessarily connected
with the idea of justice. On the other hand, this one-sided
identification of justice and equality leads to an individualistic
conception of society which, in its turn, could not but ultimately
result in a dissolution of all community. If men are essentially
equal, then they are essentially independent of each other,
every one having the essential elements of being in himself.
The conception, then, is that the association of individuals is a
merely external one, brought about only by certain tasks which
are too vast or too heavy for the individual. The egalitarian
conception of man substitutes association for community.
Association, however, is a merely arithmetical form of being
together for co-operative purposes. It is thus that Rousseau
understood community.[75] Community to him is an association
of a number of equal individuals for a certain purpose; it is not
in any way an expression of man's nature, but merely a consequence of the weakness of individual man, and therefore
something coming from outside. At the basis of this conception
we find the idea of the self-contained individual, the self-
sufficient man. It is no mere coincidence that Robinson Crusoe,
alone on his island and yet capable of having a truly human

existence, is the hero of the great novel of this era. Here is the
principle of individualism springing necessarily from the idea
of essential equality. It is at this time that all kinds of human
community begin to be understood from the point of view of
the individual, and therefore as something which is entirely
under his control.

That is why the idea of equality with its concomitant individualism—meaning by that term the essential self-sufficiency of the
individual—is the deepest cause of that decay of communal life
of which we spoke in our last lecture. The idea of equality,
taken by itself, dissolves all essential communion which is based
on a primordial togetherness of men. The place of communal
structure is usurped by inorganic association. The era of
associations has begun not only in the sense that now innumerable different associations come into existence, but also in the
more significant sense that every kind of communion is understood from the point of view of association. This is so in the
case of marriage, of the family, of the workshop, of the state.
The leading idea is Rousseau's idea of the *contrat social*. All
community life which has " grown ", all forms of communion
which have their roots in non-rational grounds are—at least in
thought—replaced by associations which are " made " and conceived of in terms of contract. Now Rousseau had already seen
that the state, being formed by the *contrat social*, is necessarily
in a condition of *révolution permanente*. A unity which is a
mere association can dissolve at any moment. There is hardly
a state which has proved the truth of Rousseau's idea more
clearly than that which was the primary result of his conception,
in which Rousseau's political ideas were incorporated, namely
the French Republic. It is the thoroughly rationalised state,
and the main elements of this rationalisation are the ideas of
equality, association and contract. The chronic crisis of parliament and government is its most visible expression. The
one-sided emphasis on equality in the conception of justice
proves to be revolutionary and ultimately anarchical.

The same is true within the sphere of economics. The idea of
equality here takes the concrete form of equal economic chances.

At first it leads to the demand for free trade, for non-interference with the free play of economic forces. It is the principle of unhampered, economic liberalism—*laissez faire*. At the same time as the feudal structure of the state, the guild-structure of economic life and all patriarchical tradition with its non-rational economic textures are broken down. Their place is taken by a completely competitive economy, which means necessarily the *bellum omnium contra omnes*, the ruthless application of the struggle for life and the survival of the fittest, the fittest meaning in this context the most cunning and the toughest. It is that kind of new economics as it was theoretically worked out in the system of the "Manchester school" of Ricardo and practically applied in the features of *Frühkapitalismus*. Even more immediate and, broadly speaking, perhaps more disastrous, the principle of equality and the individualistic idea of the *contrat social* works itself out in the realm of marriage. Marriage also is now conceived of as a *contrat social*, an association based on free-will, having its foundation in certain purposes; therefore, like every other association brought about by consent, it can also be dissolved by consent. This individualistic conception of marriage, issuing from the egalitarian conception of community, therefore means here also the *révolution permanente*, which is nothing other than that well-known and much-discussed phenomenon of our time which we call the crisis of marriage. It is not so much sexual impulse and self-indulgence, nor the general moral dissolution, but it is this idea of the *contrat social* applied to marriage which is the real cause of the enormous increase of divorce. The one-sided emphasis on equality, leading to the idea of contractual association, has proved itself in this field as well as in others as a radical element of dissolution.

However, the old paradox, that *les extrèmes se touchent*, becomes true here. Rousseau, the father of egalitarian democracy and the father of the *révolution permanente*, is also one of the originators of the totalitarian state. As a matter of fact, he gave the idea of the totalitarian state a most accurate expression by formulating the principle that the citizen creating the democratic state does so by an *aliénation totale des droits*

individuels.[76] The democratic state is conceived in terms of the
totalitarian state—which is one more proof, by the way, that
totalitarianism is not identical with dictatorship. The totalitarian state is that state which exists by force of the *aliénation
totale des droits individuels.* As Hitler's state was created by
popular vote and parliamentary decision, so is Rousseau's; but,
once created by popular vote, it is sovereign, total, irresponsible.
By the idea of *aliénation totale* the principle of " the sovereignty
of the people " becomes the principle of " the sovereignty of the
state ", which means that the state, once created democratically,
is all-powerful. The people may elect, democratically, a con-
stituent body; that duly elected group may, however, create a
constitution which is in effect the abolition of democracy. Or
the people may elect a government which, in its turn, declares
itself indissoluble and organises a totalitarian state. The principle of equality may lead to its extremest opposite, which is the
totalitarian state.

This is one road leading from equality to totalitarianism,
namely the formal, political road. The other one is economic.
The idea of equality can be understood not merely in the formal
sense of equal chances, that is, in the sense of unlimited economic
freedom; it can also be understood in a material sense, meaning
an actual equal share in the economic produce or goods. The
same idea of equality which led to the French Revolution, and
produced modern democracy, is also the source of modern
Communism. It is at the root of the concepts of Proudhon,
Marx and Lenin.

That is not so paradoxical as it appears at first sight. If we
follow the line of thought which led Marx to the construction
of his Communist system, the link between the two—extreme
anarchic Liberalism and Communism—is obvious. Marx starts
with the idea that man has lost his independence by the division
of labour which made one man dependent on the other.[77]
Division of labour, however, produced the capitalist system.
Therefore we have to reverse capitalism, and with it the division
of labour, in order to give man back his original freedom. It
is a well-known fact that Marx conceived his Communism not

as a form of state-structure, but as the abolition, or rather disappearance, of the state in a classless society. He believed that
the abolition of the class-system—which to him was identical
with the abolition of capitalism—would make the state superfluous, and would therefore automatically be followed by the
disappearance of the state. His ideal was thoroughly individualistic, based on a philosophy of absolute freedom, as we shall
see more clearly in our next lecture. But out of this individualism he developed his Communism as a means to that individual
freedom.

Unfortunately his expectation did not materialise. The first
successful Marxist revolution led to the creation of the first
totalitarian state, that of Soviet Russia, which is not only the
first, but also the most consistent, of all embodiments of the
totalitarian principle. Quite contrary to Marx's own ideal
dream, it is the case that only a Communist state can be completely totalitarian, and that all non-Communist totalitarian
states, including Hitler's, are forms of dilettante or amateurish
totalitarianism. Thus the riddle from which we started has
been solved. The same epoch which has placed the idea of
justice in the centre of interest, has also produced that social
structure which is the complete negation of all justice, the totalitarian state. The clue to this riddle is a double one: the
detachment of the idea of justice from the religious basis on the
one hand, and the identification of justice and equality on the
other.

But how are these two elements, secularism and egalitarianism, related to each other? In trying to answer this question
we turn again to the Christian idea of justice, looking at it now
from the point of view of content. We have seen that the
Church had accepted and incorporated into its own thought the
Greco-Roman idea of natural law, *lex naturae, jus naturale.* It
did so by identifying nature with God's creation and the
law of nature with God's order of creation. Now this incor-
poration also meant a transformation. That which from the
time of the Fathers, throughout the Middle Ages and the eras of
the Reformation and of Orthodoxy, was called and thought of

under the name of *jus naturale* and *lex naturae* was not the same
as Solon, Plato, Aristotle and the Stoics had understood by these
terms.   The first difference refers to the basis itself.   The Greco-
Roman concept of *lex naturae* is, of course, pantheistic: nature is
God and God is nature; therefore the law of nature is the law of
God, and the law of God is the law of nature.   This pantheistic
equation is, of course, dissolved in Christian thought.   The idea
of nature is, one might say, split into two parts: God, the
Creator, and His creation, with its God-given order.   That is to
say, God is above the order of creation.   Hence justice, being
immanent in this creation-order, is not the highest, not the ultimate principle; the highest ultimate principle is love.   For God
is Love in Himself, He is not justice in Himself.[78]   Love is His
own essence; justice, however, is His will as it refers to the order
of His created world.   That is why, in Christian thought, the
idea of justice always takes second and never first place; there is
an element of the preliminary in it.   Just as the Gospel is higher
than law, love is higher than justice.

That does not mean that justice and law are two independent
principles.   Such a dualism would be insupportable to Christian
thought.   It is rather that justice is a manifestation of love.
Justice is that love which is applied to order; love, as it can
be realised within order or structure or institution.   The origin
of all orders, and hence also the origin of justice, is like the origin
of creation as such: it is God's Love.   That is why for the
Christian the service of justice and its orders is always a service
out of love.   The motive of the Christian can never be any other
but love, even where the rule of his action has to be justice.
Justice derives from love; still it is not love in itself, but different
from love.   The unity of origin does not remove the distinction
in content, just as the distinction in content does not remove
the unity of origin.

The Christian knows that he has to serve justice, because it
is the principle of God's order; at the same time he knows that
this service of justice is not an ultimate and that respect for
justice is never sufficient as motive.   This place is reserved to
love.   With the drawing of this distinction there is already

established an enormous difference between the ancient and the Christian ideas of justice.   For the former justice is the highest, the unconditioned ideal, and service rendered to the orders of justice is the supreme task of his life.   He is incapable of conceiving anything which surpasses and transcends the idea of the just order of the world.   Because his God is not above the world-order, his ethics cannot rise above that principle which is the principle of ethical *order*, namely justice.   He does not know the God of love, therefore he does not know that love which is above justice.   The Christian, however, stands in relation to these orders of justice in the same way as he stands within this earthly existence as such, namely as one who is looking forward to a better country that is a heavenly one, to the city " whose builder and maker is God ".[79]   The Christian knows that above the demands of justice are always those of love—that he should not merely treat his neighbour as a member of an order of justice, but also, and above all, as a brother, as a man who, as a person called by God, is more than any order of justice.   Therefore he will try—and never cease to try—to bring into the orders of justice an element which is more than justice, although he knows that this love, surpassing justice, can never fit into an order and can never be expressed in terms of order and law, but only in terms of personal relationship.

The second difference concerns the content of the idea of justice, and that means its relation to the idea of equality.   In the Christian idea of justice, also, equality has its supreme importance.   All men are created by God equally in His image. They all share in this original dignity of person conferred by God.   They all have the same essential rights, based on this human dignity of God's creation.   In this affirmation of equality before God and of these original God-created rights, the Christian doctrine of justice comes close to the Stoic one.   All the same, there is a distinction between the two of no small importance. The Christian idea of rights, in distinction to the Stoic, has its reference exclusively to man and never to God.   Man has no rights over against God, being His creature and property; he lives entirely from God's grace and mercy.   Rights he has only in so far as God gives them. Therefore the rights of man are under the same reservation which applies to the whole sphere of justice. They are always limited by the unconditional imperative of love. The Roman idea, *fiat justitia pereat mundus*, is unthinkable within the Christian context.

But, above all, the Christian idea of justice is different from that of antiquity in that it gives to the element of inequality or unlikeness its due place alongside that of equality. God has created all equally in His image, but He has not created them alike; on the contrary, He has created each one different from all the rest, with his own individuality. This corresponds to the personalism of the Biblical anthropology. The human personality is based on the personal call of God. That means that everyone is created in a unique act of creation, and therefore not according to a general pattern, but as a unique individuality. While the philosophers say: *principium individuationis est materia,* the Bible says: *principium individuationis est voluntas dei creatoris.* The differences between human beings are therefore not irrelevant, casual, immaterial, but just as much God's will and creation as the equality of personal dignity.

The elements of equality and unlikeness, however, do not stand on the same level. In Christ Jesus all differences, and therefore all individuality, become irrelevant. "There is neither Jew nor Greek, there is neither bond nor free, there is neither male nor female: for ye are all one in Christ Jesus."[80] This is the eschatological, and therefore the final, point of view. It is within this earthly, preliminary existence that these differences are to be acknowledged and taken seriously. It is here that the preliminary principle of justice is valid. There shall be a time when justice gives way to love, when the law shall be superseded, when all the earthly conditions and limitations shall no longer exist. Then the individual differences will play no rôle, but till then they have to be acknowledged as God's will for this earthly existence. God has given to every one his own " face "; that is why unlikeness comes into the idea of justice.

Of course, the fact of the unlikeness of man was not unknown to the philosophers of antiquity, but from this fact they drew conclusions which have to be repudiated from the point of view of Biblical thought. They drew one of two conclusions. In older Greek philosophy, as represented by Plato and Aristotle, the unlikeness of man is the foundation of a different claim. The unlikeness is primarily understood as a different participation in reason. Greeks have more reason than the barbarians; men have more reason than women; the slaves have none at all. They have to be treated accordingly; that means that the difference of men limits their equality of dignity and rights. The later Stoics have another view. Their conception of man is dominated by the idea of equality and equal dignity in such a measure that they have no interest at all in unlikeness. It seems to them something irrelevant, casual, not worth taking seriously. That is to say, the principle of equality encroaches upon unlikeness. It is the exact reverse of the older view.

In Christian thought, however, the two elements of equality and unlikeness are not in competition with each other and do not limit each other, because they are on a different plane. Men are equal in their relation to God, and therefore in their dignity. They are unlike in their individuality, and therefore in their function in the created world. There is but one and the same dignity for all, just as theirs is only one and the same destiny whether they are men or women, children or adults, black or white, whether they are strong or weak, intelligent or dull. Their final destiny being the same, their personal dignity cannot but be the same. All the same, the individual differences are not negligible. What God has created cannot be irrelevant or negligible. The difference of individuality involves a difference of the function within society.

Finally the two elements—equality and unlikeness, equal dignity and different function—are combined in such a way that both get their full expression in the Christian idea of communion. Because men are different from each other, they are also dependent on each other. Man needs woman in order to be entirely man; woman needs man in order to be entirely woman. This unlikeness points towards mutual completion and co-operation. Individuals are different, like the limbs of the body, each one having its own function for which it is fitted by its individuality. The difference of function necessarily creates a somewhat hierarchical order in service, which again rests on the difference of individuality. According to his make-up, the one is fit for a subordinate, the other for a superior position, the one for a more extraverted, the other for a more intraverted function. In this way the function of woman in marriage and family is entirely different from that of man, and the function of the children entirely different from that of the parents. This difference, or unlikeness, in kind and function is exactly the unity of the family as a community. It is so because this difference in no ways encroaches upon the equal dignity. Functional subordination has nothing whatever to do with lesser dignity or person. Society is thought of as a community of unlike individuals, who are bound to each other by the necessity of mutual completion and united by mutual respect for their equal dignity. We might call this idea an organic conception of society, but, in doing so, we must distinguish it clearly from that conception of organic unity which we find in a certain Romantic philosophy. For this Romantic organology lacks that element which is decisive within the Christian understanding of society, namely equality of personal dignity. Within Romantic thought the person is subordinated to the social whole by some kind of mystical principle of a *Gesamtpersönlichkeit*. The Romantic conception is totalitarian or collectivist, robbing human personality of its finality.

This, then, is the unique character of the Christian idea of society and of justice: that it combines the two principal elements of equality and unlikeness which everywhere else are in conflict with each other. It is this combination of the transcendental and the psychological, of the personal and the functional aspect, which gives the Christian idea of justice a flexibility, a dialectical subtlety, which no other has. It is neither egalitarian nor authoritarian, it is organic and, nonetheless, spiritual. It combines the naturalistic evaluation of different individuality and functional subordination with the most unconditional acknowledgment of the finality of every person. Now this combination of elements, and therefore this idea of justice which excludes both individualism and collectivism, authoritarianism and egalitarianism, is essentially and exclusively Christian. It is the Christian conception of divine creation—creation by the individual call of God to the universal destiny of all—which makes this possible and necessary. Apart from its basis in Christianity, this combination is possible only as a matter of chance without any inner necessity.

That is why the progressive estrangement of modern society from Christian thinking inevitably entailed the consequences which we have seen. It created first an individualistic and egalitarian liberalism, which led to latent or open anarchy. This evoked the reaction of collectivism which, by destroying human personality, destroyed the foundation of justice in the totalitarian dictatorship. Without Christian faith and Christian understanding of justice the world faces, therefore, a fatal alternative: either humanity tries to return to, or to preserve, an individualistic liberalism defending the rights of man, but leading to the destruction of community, or it goes on along the road of totalitarian collectivism, organising community by the complete effacement of personality. There *is* a middle road, namely the combination of personal finality and functional structure which derives its inner coherence entirely and exclusively from the Christian faith, or to be more exact, from the Christian conception of justice, based in that of creation. By this Christian conception of justice, personal life is the supreme value and is to be defended against all totalitarian collectivist encroachments. On the other hand, this highest evaluation of individual personality does not lead to an individualism which has no understanding of essential social unity. The true Christian faith does hold the key to the solution of the social problems of our time, so far as there is any solution within this sinful world. The question is whether humanity will use this key or whether it prefers to continue in the direction of recent centuries, to its utter ruin.

APPENDIX TO LECTURE VIII

Justice, Tradition and Patriarchalism

It seems to me to be justifiable and even necessary to deal here with a number of questions which were raised in several discussions which this lecture on justice evoked:—

1. The relation of egalitarianism to tradition. It has been observed by many that in England—as well as in Switzerland—the deep-rooted liberalism and individualism of the people has not produced the same dangerous quasi-anarchical effects which can be seen in other democratic countries, as, for instance, France; and it was often pointed out that this difference is accounted for by the strong sense of tradition in the first, which is lacking in so many other countries. But, so far as I know, the inherent relation between egalitarianism and the lack of tradition has never been made quite clear.

Rationalistic egalitarianism is necessarily anti-traditional because it claims equal right for any present decision with anything that has been decided previously. An existing parliament, elected by the people yesterday, has the right to upset to-day what has been decided in previous times by previous parliaments, kings, or similar powers. Egalitarianism tends to the atomisation of time, as it tends to the atomisation of communal society. It is, so to speak, an individualism of the time elements on the basis of the equal right of any given time. Why should that which previous generations have decided be binding for me, for us, at this moment? Tradition—the assertion of continuity—is a non-rational principle, sometimes irrational, sometimes suprarational, but, in any case, not to be accounted for in rational terms. Behind the emphasis on tradition stands a conception of man which is anti-individualistic, giving preponderance to the continuum of the generations over against the isolated present generation. It is the conviction of the traditionalist that the wisdom of past times, embedded in tradition, is greater than the wisdom of the present generation, taken by itself.

A similar idea is expressed in that system of checks and balances which is the basic idea of that marvellous piece of political wisdom known to us as the constitution of the United States, and—still more so—of the constitution of Switzerland, which is only partly modelled on the American.   In both cases the egalitarian, rational element is counterbalanced by elements which allow past decisions to limit the freedom of decision of the present, and upon which rests the stability of the whole political structure.   The interplay of the rational and individualistic principle of equality with the non-rational and non-individual-istic principle of tradition, or of checks and balances by past decisions, is the clue to the mystery of the comparative stability of these three democracies in comparison with those which are based entirely on the rational principle of equality.   If we ask where this difference comes from, I think the answer cannot be in doubt.   It is the strength of the Christian tradition in all these countries—at the time when their present structure was formed—which accounts for this curious check on the egalitarian principle.

2. Some critics of the lecture on justice seemed to be afraid that its emphasis on the anti-egalitarian principle of unlikeness might lead to a conservative patriarchalism.   They objected particularly to applying the functional principle to the power of the state.   As often happens, if one mentions several arguments in support of an accepted opinion and one only against it, the former are apt to be overlooked and attention only given to the one.   It should be clear from what was said in the lecture that the principle of equality was put in the first rank, and adequate reason was given for doing so.   But our age is so dominated by the egalitarian principle that even a hint at the fact that it might not be the whole of wisdom is enough to arouse suspicion of authoritarianism.   I do not say that the family, with its parental authority, is the pattern for all social order.   I am quite aware of the fact that the basis of the family is the " unlikeness " of the child with the adult which places upon the parents a responsibility *for* the child, which is never the responsibility *of* the child.   This is the *specific* unlikeness which is characteristic

of the family community. Therefore the specific structure of the family ought not to be taken as the model for other structures where *this* unlikeness does not enter. What I do say, however, is that unlikeness of *some* kind occurs in all communities and ought to be taken into consideration as a positive and not as a negative factor, being God's creation. A workshop or factory is not a family, because the workers' relation to the employer is not that of immature children to the adult parents. On the other hand, we feel without much reflection that it would be a good thing if the workshop or factory was a little more like a family than it is now. It is not, in this good sense, a family exactly, because the *merely* contractual relationship makes that impossible. What I plead for is that it should not be a *merely* contractual association but *more* of a family-like unity, and that this comes about only by giving due consideration to the "organic" principle of community, based *not only* on equality but *also* on unlikeness. The *contrat-social* idea is at the basis of the class-struggle, because contractual association will always be a competitive unit. Those who see the necessity of overcoming the class-struggle by other means than those devised by Karl Marx should be interested in finding an alternative to *mere* contractual association. This is, if I am not wrong, the tendency within that sector of the trade-union movement which has become suspicious of both the old liberal and the new collectivist model.

3. As far as the application of this conception of justice to the state is concerned, the essentials have been outlined in my opening lecture. There are two kinds of democracy: the rational democracy of Rousseau and the Christian idea, including both the rational element of equality and the non-rational element of tradition and essential or organic community. It is true that political power is not primarily to be understood as "function". Political power, ultimate decision over life and death, is a unique problem, and its norms are different from those of any other community. But it is just for this reason that the one-sided emphasis on equality in this sphere is particularly obnoxious. It works either in the direction of instability, by the rigorous

application of the principle of the *sovereignty of the people*, or in the opposite direction of totalitarianism, by the principle of the *sovereignty of the state*. Furthermore, it does not afford any safeguard against the first turning into the second. That is why this egalitarian element needs the check of the non-rational element of tradition and of those instruments which provide for the influence of past decision over present decision or, negatively, for a certain independence of political power from the present will of the people and its representatives. That is what is meant by the principle of political authority. The British Parliament, the American Congress and the Swiss Nationalversammlung are not all-powerful. They are checked by tradition and constitution, by the President, or by the Federal Government, which, at any given moment, are independent of the present will of Parliament. This is the non-rational foundation of political authority which, as such, is the perpetual target for the criticism of the rationalists, who stake all their political wisdom on the principle of equality.

4. There is, however, another feature of political life in which the non-rational, non-egalitarian idea takes shape, namely the federal structure of the state. Rationalism is centralistic, but the Christian concept works toward federalism, *i.e.* a political structure which is not built on the principle of mere " delegation from the top ", but on the representative principle, or " delegation from below ". For the rationalist, the small units are mere organs of the central will; for the federalist, on the other hand, the central power is a mere superstructure above more or less autonomous small units. In centralism, the individual is faced directly with the central power of the state, the intermediates being mere organs of the central power. In federalism, however, there are, between the individual and the central power, a number of semi-autonomous intermediates of different kinds, such as local communities, cantons, corporations and trade unions. Whilst centralism is the direct outcome of the principle of equality, federalism is the outcome of that combination of equality and unlikeness for which we are pleading. In the first case the principle of the majority vote is everything; in the

second case it is checked by the will not to admit the principle of majority and minority at all where the major interests of a local smaller unit are concerned. Switzerland is probably the only country in which this non-rational principle is carried through consistently, and where at the same time it is combined with the rational principle of the majority vote based on equality. And this has been the secret of the stability of that country and its immunity from the totalitarian germ.

IX

THE PROBLEM OF FREEDOM

THE idea of freedom is not one of those which, like the ideas of truth and justice, have stirred humanity throughout all the ages. As a *guiding* idea and a *basic* principle of human existence, it is the product of modern times. It is true that within the New Testament message reference is made to freedom, but no one would claim that this idea holds a key-position. It will be our task to search out the reason for this. But for the moment attention should be called to the fact that the word freedom is used with very different meanings. Freedom occurs in the most different contexts, in different layers, so to speak, of our existence. Perhaps we shall understand this best if we start with the opposite idea, of unfreedom. Man is unfree when he has no room to decide and shape his life. The maximum of this unfreedom is represented by the condition of the slave, whose whole life is in the hands of another, and who cannot dispose either of his time or of his powers, who has to do continuously what another forces him to do. Now this slavery, in the old classical sense of the word, has ceased to be a problem of our society, but it may be questioned with good reason whether unfreedom is less acute and less dangerous when the place of the individual slave-owner is taken by the commanding power of a state, which determines life and action in the same comprehensive manner, leaving almost no room for individual decision. The rise of totalitarian states has given the problem of freedom a tremendous new actuality, not because it is dictatorship, *i.e.* not because it prevents the individual citizen from sharing in the decision of government, but because such a state, whatever form it takes, controls the individual in all sections of his life, leaving almost no sphere for private activity, responsibility and planning, prescribing all that the individual must do and not do, must say and not say, commanding where he is to live and to work, and making an individual negative utterance or decision a matter of capital punishment. In the totalitarian state the individual, like a remotely controlled aeroplane, is directed in all his movements by the will and commands of the state.

We are proud, and rightly so, of our democratic freedoms. But we are not always sufficiently conscious of the extent to which the majority of citizens are under the dictate of another's will, even in our free countries. It is true, they have the formal freedom to do or not to do what they like or dislike within the wide limits of that which the state demands and prohibits as a minimum. But this state-free space is occupied by other directing powers; the worker is forced to take work where it is offered, he is forced to take it under the conditions which are offered to him; the free contract is more or less a fiction. Whoever is not independent by reason of considerable wealth must do a multitude of things which he would not do if he were not compelled to. And he cannot do many things which he would do if he could. Nobody eats poor food voluntarily, nobody lives in bad houses voluntarily, very few voluntarily forgo the pleasures which they see enjoyed by others. The power restricting a man's will in all these cases is money. That is, the lack of money prevents man from doing and having what he wants to do and to have. Here, as well as in the case of the state, it is man-made institutions that limit and narrow down the area of freedom for the non-privileged to such an extent that the space of free decision seems not so very much larger than in the totalitarian state.

There is a space, however, which no state, no social order, no slave-owner of any kind can narrow down and that is the area of inner freedom. Nobody can prevent me from thinking, believing, loving, hating, hoping and fearing as I wish. That is why the slave, Epictetus, was able to affirm his freedom; he had discovered the illimitable realm of inwardness, compared with which all the external dependence, implied in his being a slave, seemed irrelevant. In a similar way the Apostle Paul exhorted the slave members of the community of Corinth [81] not to struggle to get rid of their fetters, because they were in possession of a freedom so great and lasting that, compared with it, this outward unfreedom would seem irrelevant.

But how about this inward freedom? Are we really free to think and to will and to judge as we want to, to give our action the direction which we decide? Are there not also powers that limit this inward area of freedom and perhaps reduce it to nothing. The Bible, as you know, speaks of the slavery of sin, of inward powers dominating man's will and driving his thought, feeling and action in a direction against his will and which hold him back from what he does will.[82] Again, there is a certain philosophy that goes even further and declares freedom to be entirely illusory. It says that man is always like that remotely controlled aeroplane; that his interior life, his thinking and willing, is never free, but always determined by his nature, his inborn character, his physical constitution, by the functioning of his glands and the effect of the hormones. The action of man, even if he seems to be his own lord and master, is no freer than the trajectory of a bullet shot by a gun. Again, it is said, man is not free in his thinking and willing because he is always a child of his time, a product of his environment, a particle of that historical stream in which, *nolens volens*, he has to swim.

In order to find our way in this perplexing multitude of facts and conceptions of freedom, let us make an initial distinction. There are two separate problems of freedom, quite distinct from each other. First, how far and in what sense *is* man free or unfree? Second, how far and in what sense *ought* man to be free? It will be seen in our later discussion that these two questions, utterly distinct as they are at first sight, are in close connection with each other. At first, however, the distinction— even the separation—of the two is necessary. The question whether man is free, and to what degree, is answered in extremely different ways, some of the answers affirming a perfect freedom, the others denying any kind of freedom. The first of these two extremes, the idealism of freedom, is a very exceptional

phenomenon compared with the second—determinism. Apart
from the philosophy of Fichte,[83] the boldest form of liberalism—
the assertion of absolute freedom—has hardly ever been formulated. This doctrine becomes possible only by denying the
reality of an outward world that could and would necessarily
limit freedom: because, and in so far as the self or Ego creates the
non-Ego, the outward world, it can be unconditionally free; that
means that this Ego or self is identified with God. On this condition only can absolute freedom be affirmed. It is easily
understood that this extreme liberalism had no great chance of
becoming popular. It remains to be seen whether the renewal of
this theory of absolute freedom has any better chance in its most
recent atheistic form, in the so-called existentialism of Sartre.

The closest approximation to Fichte seems to be the Vedanta
philosophy of identity, teaching the identity of Brahma, the
One and All, with Atman, the principle of selfhood. But,
strange as it appears to us Europeans, the idea of freedom is here
completely overshadowed by the idea of being. Indian thought
is not interested in the problem of freedom at all. At the other
extreme we find determinism, the doctrine of complete unfreedom, which—in distinction from the former doctrine—has
a great following, particularly in our time, even amongst those
who have never bothered much about philosophical questions,
and who would not be capable of doing so. This determinism
may be a very simple but thoroughgoing conviction, expressed in
the phrase: *Ich bin nun einmal so!*—" I cannot help being what
I am!"—a phrase which one can hear both from the most highly
educated as well as the simplest, and which expresses a complete
determinism. Being a self is understood entirely on the analogy
of objective being. Just as a lump of lead "is what it is" because
of the number of molecules and their atomic particles, so man is
determined by his constitution; his self is the sum of phycho-
logical or physical factors and his designs are the resultant of the
different components as they arise from the psycho-physical
structure of man and the reciprocal action and reaction between
him and his outward world. Freedom, then, is nothing but the
constitutionally determined possibility of reaction to the outward

world. Although this conception as a theory has many adherents, practically it does not play a great rôle. The determinist lives almost always as if he were not a determinist, and in his dealings with others he presupposes that they are not determined, but have a certain measure of freedom.

And this, whether with or without philosophical formulation, is the view of the majority of people. Man has a certain measure of freedom from physical heritage and constitution, from environment and historical streams; he is a self-deciding, responsible being. It is surprising and comforting to find how little this untheoretical, unreasoned, and even unconscious conviction of freedom and responsibility is affected or shaken by adverse theory.

The Christian conception of freedom links up with this middle view between determinism and indeterminism. The problem of free-will, which plays such a rôle in philosophy, is hardly mentioned in the Bible. The freedom and unfreedom of man are lifted from the theoretical field into that of practical God-relation. The freedom of man is presupposed as a matter of course, because, and in so far as, man is seen as always responsible to God. Man is a subject who has to decide and to act, and is obliged to give account for what he does. On the other hand, man is free only in a very limited sense since he is a creature. He is placed as an individual subject within space and time. My space and my time are also my limits. Above all, my being bound to a physical body reminds me of the limitation of my freedom.

But this creaturely limitation, as such, does not infringe upon that freedom which is essential for man, and which is primarily realised in his responsibility before God. In being created in God's image he has received dominion over the other creatures. It is in this superiority over the sub-human nature, and the physical world, that man experiences his aboriginal freedom: "Thou hast put all things under his feet".[84] The specific character of the Christian idea of freedom is, however, founded in the fact that man's freedom springs from the same spot from which comes his dependence. His freedom has its real possibility only within this dependence on God, so that the maximum of dependence on God is the maximum of his freedom, and that any attempt to get out of the dependence on God leads to slavery.

For ordinary thinking—whether of a more idealistic or materialistic, deterministic or indeterministic brand—freedom is identical with independence. Whether this freedom is affirmed, denied or postulated, freedom is in clear opposition to dependence. Man is free so far as he is independent, he is un-free so far as he is dependent. That is the axiomatic, rational conception of freedom inherent in so-called common sense. Either free or dependent: so far as dependence goes, freedom is excluded; so far as freedom goes, dependence is excluded.

This common-sense idea of freedom originates in our reflection on our relation to the world. With regard to the world and to nature it is valid. But this conception of freedom does not grasp the centre of personality. The centre of personality is our relation to God. In our relation to God, however, this either/or, which is true in relation to the world, ceases to be true and becomes the very opposite of truth. For in relation to God man is the more free as he is the more dependent. *Deo servire libertas*. The human self is not an entity in itself. Human personality is what it is through its relation to God. Man is a true self or person, and therefore he has freedom in so far as he is not " in himself " or " by himself ", but in God, *i.e.* in so far as he does not determine himself, but lets himself be determined by God. Here, then, is the opposite of *autarky* or self-sufficiency. The more man is sufficient unto himself, the less he is free; and the less he suffices for himself and seeks his life and meaning in God, the freer he is.[85]

In the Bible this attempt of man to withdraw himself from God, to be sufficient unto himself and to become independent of his Creator, is called sin. And this sin is consequently and truthfully connected with unfreedom or slavery. Man's attempt to emancipate himself from God does not end merely in misery, but in the loss of freedom. That is the meaning of the doctrine of the fall of the first men. Adam and Eve let themselves be so hoodwinked as to seek their freedom in independence of God. They are the prototypes of modern man; they thought to become free by becoming independent, by throwing off the tie which bound them to God. They thought by doing so to become like God, absolutely free, independent selves grounded in themselves, and therefore having their freedom in themselves.

Man, desiring to become free in the sense of being independent of God, confuses God and the world; he wants to be independent of God as he ought to be independent of the world. But by cutting himself loose from God in order to become free, he loses the stand from which he can be free with regard to the world. He loses that Archimedean fulcrum outside the world by which he really could move the world. By cutting himself loose from God, man precipitates himself into the world and becomes its prisoner. Man liberated from God becomes the slave of the world. Without his noticing it, the world becomes his God, theoretically and practically. Theoretically, man makes the world God by absolutising it and giving it the attributes of divinity. Practically, he does the same thing by surrendering himself totally to the world and what the world has to give. "Every imagination of the thoughts of his heart" is filled with the world, but never satisfied. The soul of man, created for God, can never be satisfied with finite things. That is why, cut off from God and lost in the world, it is insatiable and ever disappointed. Moreover, the world attracts him with a force that is not merely the force of sensual stimulation, but of a demonic power, absolutised finiteness. He is not merely the slave of the world, but the slave of the demons.

From this point we can understand the development of the problem of freedom in the modern age. By throwing overboard the Christian conception of freedom, two alternatives are developed—a false liberalism on the one side, a false determinism on the other—which, in spite of their being opposites in many ways, merge into one another. On the one hand, the conception of freedom as independence produces a rational liberalism, which reaches its summit in Fichte: the self is identical with God, and this self creates the world. It is quite logical that Fichte should see the Biblical idea of creation as the first criterion of false philosophy and as the origin of metaphysical error.[56] The self is itself the creator—how should there be a creator above it? This extreme liberalism, carrying the identification of freedom with independence to its last consequence, was too bold to acquire much following. A closely related idea, however, became the starting point of one of the most powerful movements of the last century.

At the basis of Karl Marx's system we find the idea of freedom identified with independence. Marx teaches a kind of fall of humanity, an initial point of the erroneous development, and a source of all the evils from which modern society suffers. This fatal beginning is the loss of independence, taking place, first, within the economic reality by the division of labour, and, second, in its ideological consequence, in the recognition of a God. Marx formulates this axiom: " Man is free only if he owes his existence to himself ".[57] Therefore the recognition of a God, being identical with the loss of independence, is the beginning of unfreedom. Therefore mankind can regain its freedom only by shaking off this double dependence, i.e. by overcoming the capitalist division of labour through Communism and by shaking off religion. In the classless society man owes his existence to himself, and in atheism he becomes aware of the fact that he owes it to himself. Therefore Communism and atheism are linked together in the very foundations of the Marxist system, in the same way as capitalism is linked together with belief in God. The abolition of capitalism is at the same time the abolition of religion. The two are two sides of the same process of regaining liberty, which is independence.

We find a similar idea expressed in what Nikolai Hartmann, the Berlin philosopher, calls postulatory atheism. For the sake of liberty the non-existence of God must be postulated, because the acknowledgment of God is irreconcilable with independence. Again, we find a very seductive variation of this idea in a little work by André Gide, L'enfant prodigue, in which the author interprets the parable of the prodigal son by consciously turning it in the opposite direction. The prodigal son was quite right to emancipate himself from his father; that is how he became a free man.

More impressive than all these expressions of postulatory atheism is that of Friedrich Nietzsche. To him also the idea of God represents, so to speak, a fall of humanity. For it is the belief in a God which makes possible the uprising of the weak against the strong. The fictitious thought: "There is a God, father of all men", produces that slave morality of service and paralyses the will-to-power on the part of the powerful. By the idea of God, the Lilliputian men, the powerless herd people, enslave and fetter the great and powerful individuals and prevent them from doing what is, according to the true principle of life, according to the doctrine of the will-to-power, the right thing to do: to use their power and to dominate the weak. None has ever expressed this postulatory atheism more bluntly than Nietzsche's Zarathustra. "If there were Gods, who could bear not to be a God? Therefore there are no Gods." Atheism is the product of the will to absolute independence. It is Nietzsche who has expressed the thought which, according to the Genesis narrative, stirred only half-consciously in the soul of Adam and Eve, but was what the serpent meant by saying: *Eritis sicut deus*.

False liberalism is the one, false determinism is the other line which European thought took in cutting loose from the Christian idea of freedom. While radical liberalism says, "There is no God", because there is—or there ought to be— human freedom, radical determinism says, "There is no freedom, because there is no God". Radical determinism is pancausalism; pancausalism is elimination of God. If there is no God, there is only world. If there is world only, everything is determined by that category which is the very definition of the world, causality. Because there is world only, there cannot be freedom. Man, also, is a particle of the world, a tiny wheel in this machinery of the world. Freedom is an illusion, because God is an illusion. Man is an object amongst objects, a particularly complicated object, of which the most essential element is his brain. Man is fixed by his constitution just as a machine is fixed by its construction. Here it becomes apparent that man is precipitated into the world by losing his hold in God. He is not in any degree removed from it; he is entirely submerged in it.

Even more important than the metaphysical question of freedom and determinism is the ethical question about what kind of freedom man ought to have. The history of the last few centuries shows an almost uninterrupted chain of movements of freedom or emancipation. The idea of freedom is—alongside that of equality—the strongest spiritual driving force in the life of modern Western humanity. The first of those movements of liberation is a process which has rarely been seen from this angle, namely the evolution of modern technics as the sub-conscious attempt of man to free himself from his dependence on nature. In a gigantic wrestling-match with the forces of nature, man tries to become her master. This idea previously inspired the alchemists of the time of the Renaissance human-ism. They were seeking the philosopher's stone which would give them magical power over the forces of nature. It is not modern science which has produced modern technics, but it is this will, subconscious rather than conscious, to elevate oneself above the dependence of creaturely being which accounts for the vehemence of the scientific as well as the technical enthusiasm of the modern age. That is why technique so often preceded science and showed it the way.[88] But it is only in the last phase of this development that this motive came to the surface and unveiled itself completely as technocratical pseudo-religion. Here it becomes clear that the deepest source of this movement is rebellion against the Creator, but a rebellion which clothes itself in a pseudo-religious garment. The credo of this religion is: We do not need a God any longer, since by science and technics we have become Gods ourselves. The attribute of omnipotence and saving power is transferred from God to organised humanity.

On the tombstone of Benjamin Franklin we find the inscription, more characteristic of his admirers than of himself: "He wrested the lightning from heaven and the sceptre from the tyrants ". The liberation-movement of political revolution is seen together with an emancipation-movement in the direction of the transcendent. It is again the motive of Prometheus; through his technical knowledge man becomes independent not only of nature, but of deity. Whilst it was fitting for the man of antiquity to take refuge from the whims of nature in prayer, this seems no longer possible or worthy of the man who can split the atom and has the unlimited secret powers of nature at his disposal.

It is fair to add, however, that the idea of technical omnipotence in our days does not so much bewitch the minds of the masters and pioneers of science and scientific technics as it does the younger generation and those nations for which science and technics are comparatively new. The more mature minds have become aware that mankind is now in the situation of the Sorcerer's Apprentice of Goethe, who by the stolen magic word of his master forced into his service the slave-spirits, but could not really rule them, so that he finally found himself in great danger of being ruined by their very service. There are many amongst the scientific masters of our time who confess with no little apprehension that technical knowledge has outgrown the control of man and that it is no more a serviceable spirit, but has become a master dangerous to life. Why is that the case? Because man has developed his life on the lines of emancipation from God, in the foolish belief that freedom is independence, and now learns from bitter experience, what he could have known from the Bible, that this independence is not freedom but slavery, endangering his life.

We can see equally clearly the same thing at work in the liberation-movements taking place in the sphere of political and social life. When modern man speaks of liberty, he first of all thinks of political and social freedom. Now, in the Christian conception of human life, there is a marvellous balance of freedom and dependence in human relation, because freedom and dependence are already tied together in the root of man's personal existence, in his relation to God.[89] Truly, man is called by God to freedom. He who is a servant of God is a free man amongst men. The Creator has made man free; slavery is a negation of God's order of creation. The unconditional commandment of love protects everyone from the claim to dominion on the part of the others. Equal dignity includes equal freedom. But now you will remember that in the Christian conception of man there is founded not only this equal dignity, from which mutual independence derives, but also unlikeness, from which mutual dependence follows. Man is not created only for freedom but also for community, and not only for the free community of love, but also for functional interdependence, which is based on the principle of supplementation and the structural subordination of each individual within a functional unit. The Biblical principle of life does not establish *autarky* but mutual giving and receiving; not the individualistic existence of Robinson Crusoe, but marriage, family, neighbourly community and political solidarity.

Now, in this functional unity there is always a subordination alongside equal dignity. The one must be above, the other below; the one must lead, the other obey. Wherever men have to do something together, there must be a hierarchy of competence, of command; where this is not recognised, the co-operative unit falls to pieces. This hierarchy is also an order of creation, but it must be distinguished most strictly from that kind of hierarchy which includes inequality of dignity and of freedom. This functional order of co-operation is, however, always falsified by man's egoism, which transforms functional structure and service into some kind of caste-system or class-rule, enslaving and degrading large parts of mankind. In order to increase the power and profit of the privileged, a false system of authority is erected which destroys liberty. This was the situation at the beginning of the modern era. The liberation-movement had as its purpose and legitimate aim to destroy this false order of authority, as it was incorporated in feudalism and in the ecclesiastical hierarchy. The battle had to be fought in the name of God-given freedom. But the fact that this battle was also to be fought against a false Church authority gave rise to the deep misunderstanding that a battle had to be fought against the authority of God as such. The rationalist interpretation of equality implied suspicion of any kind of authority and professed that any kind of subordination was contrary to human dignity and freedom. The very concept of authority was discredited in the name of freedom. It was by this misunderstanding that the idea of freedom became the lever of the anarchical destruction of society.

Within this process we have to distinguish three phases. In the first, liberalism of the idealistic type still recognised a certain transcendent root of human dignity, and therefore a certain divine authority, the authority of a categorical imperative or moral law. But this authority was uncertain because, by the principle of autonomy, this moral law was interpreted as our own law, and therefore real dependence and authority were not acknowledged as they are implied in the faith in a creator. Moral law was interpreted in such a way that the idea of authority vanished in the light of the idea of freedom.[90] While the authority of a transcendent power thus becomes uncertain, the idea of authority among men disappears altogether. There is no further place for that natural interdependence forming structural units. All community is understood merely as society. Authority among men is merely provided for in the attenuated form of " administration ", as it is grounded in the idea that the freedom of the one has to be limited by the freedom of the other. This is the idea of the *contrat social* of which we spoke in the last lecture. Contractual association is substituted for original community. Authority is merely the delegation of individual rights. Government becomes administration which has to execute the will of the sovereign people, whether good or evil, and this, again, is justified by the assumption that the will of the people is always good.

In the second phase even the transcendental element which remained within idealism, namely the divine moral law, disappears. There is no more moral authority, there is only freedom without authority. The attempt is now made to construct society and state on the principle of freedom alone, in such a way that all social order and rule is considered as a mere measure of utility. This is the condition of *laissez faire*, of the utmost possible limitation and progressive diminution of legal authority, the proclamation of free love superseding the out-moded institution of marriage.

The third phase is a reaction against the anarchical state of society into which *laissez faire* liberalism had thrown it. It has become apparent that society cannot exist without authority holding it together. But no authority of a spiritual character is left—neither that of a moral law, nor that of God. One has to create an authority of a bluntly *de facto* character, the authority of the one who has the power, *i.e.* dictatorship on a purely naturalistic basis. It is evident that this dictatorship is irreconcilable with those rights of man that were proclaimed in previous centuries, because these rights would make this *de facto* authority uncertain and might destroy it. Therefore this very freedom has to be attacked and it is attacked, not always quite without reason, as individualistic and a danger to society. The totalitarian state despises, ridicules and discredits liberal democracy, basing its criticism on the shortcomings inherent in individualistic liberalism. Individual freedom disappears in the collectivist totalitarian state, which is erected not on a moral foundation but on sheer power. And this, so far, is the end of those modern movements of liberation in which freedom was understood as independence, and which could not but fulfil the warning word that the Creator spoke to Adam: " For in the day that thou eatest thereof thou shalt surely die ".

We said in the beginning that the idea of freedom is not at the centre of Biblical revelation. Freedom, rightly understood, is not the first, but a second word. The first word is dependence on God, God's lordship. First comes God's gift and will. God gives freedom to man in binding him to Himself. Man's freedom is identical with his dependence on God: " If the Son therefore shall make you free, ye shall be free indeed ".[91] " Where the Spirit of the Lord is, there is liberty!" [92] It was the tragic error of modern humanity to seek a freedom outside of and in independence of God. This way could not but lead into the opposite, into slavery, be it slavery to the world or slavery under man's dominion.

Where freedom is not sought in independence, but in dependence on God, there the mastery over things will not lead to obsession by the things of the world or by technical powers; there the freedom of the individual will not produce the dissolution of community; there the structural hierarchy of competence based on unlikeness will not lead to an authoritarian caste-system or class-dominion; there individual freedom and social cohesion will be balanced, because the recognition of equal dignity is combined with a functional aristocracy, the freedom of the individual and the interest of the community being equally recognised.

Let us remember, however, with reference to freedom, what has been said in previous connections: that the false directions of the emancipation-movements of modern times had their origin not merely in the rebellion against divine authority, but also in the legitimate rebellion against false authority, for which empirical Christianity was responsible either indirectly or directly. Not only had the Church sanctioned the misuse of authority by the political and economic powers, but it had itself created a clerical system of false authority and in its orthodoxy false spiritual authorities, which in the long run were insupportable. Therefore Christianity still faces the task of interpreting the Christian message in such a way that freedom of the individual, as well as the order of society, is grounded in unconditional dependence on God.

X

THE PROBLEM OF CREATIVITY

ALL culture lives by the creative powers of the human mind. For culture is that which man does beyond biological necessity. It is the sum of the new things which nature does not and cannot furnish. This creative power —talent or, at its maximum, genius—is in itself something bestowed. Man cannot produce talent or genius. Talent or genius cannot be made by education. Either you have this power or you do not have it. Education, training, schooling of any kind may assist the talent, and the lack of these or other unfavourable conditions may hinder or even destroy the creative powers; but in themselves they are, as the word genius indicates, given by birth. You cannot decide to be or to become a genius; either you are one by birth, or you will never be. This factor, then—the factor of creative power, talent or genius—belongs to those nature-given elements of civilisation or culture which from the beginning we have been leaving out of our consideration.

Two things, however, lie decidedly within the range of our interest, *i.e.* within that area where religious faith or unbelief becomes relevant. First, the direction which is given to the use of these creative powers; and second, the place and rank which is given to them within our whole system of values and our conception of the meaning of human existence at large. By being a Christian, or a pagan, or an atheist, one does not become a person of greater or smaller talent. Faith, unbelief, a world-outlook on this or that order neither enhances nor diminishes genius. But certainly the fact of being a Christian or a non-Christian, a true believer or an atheist, expresses itself in the direction which creativity takes. And further, faith or unbelief, world-outlook of any kind, must and will emerge in very different conceptions and evaluations of the creative element within the totality of human life. These, then, are the two problems with which we have to deal in trying to grasp the relations between Christian faith and cultural life.

It is only in a comparatively late phase of the evolution of the human mind that man becomes conscious of his creative powers. At first, and for a long while, it is only his physical creativity which attracts his interest. In the Phallus- and Lingam-cult he venerates his sexual creativity as a divine power. Later on, it is the formation of the state and legislation in which he sees the manifestation of supernatural divine forces. Again, in a later stage, he becomes conscious of the different $\tau\acute{\epsilon}\chi\nu\eta$, the crafts and arts, the use of fire, the handling of metals, agriculture, and finally the liberal arts, as being expressions of specifically human nature, of his creative powers.

But now it is striking and most significant that the evaluation of this cultural creativity is not naively positive, but reflected and complex. The myth of Prometheus is a characteristic expression of this complex view. Certainly Prometheus, the titanic hero who taught men the crafts and arts and brought them the fire from heaven out of compassion, is a benefactor, but at the same time he is a rebel against a divine order. He had to steal the fire from the gods and for that underwent terrible punishment. That is, according to this view the rise of the creative capacity of man is looked at somehow suspiciously, as if there were something unlawful about it. It is somehow a product of usurpation. Although man is delighted to have all these faculties, he is still conscious of a tension which, because he has them, exists between creative man and the divine order. A similar feeling seems to be expressed in Germanic mythology, where it is the dark demi-gods of the underworld who possess the secret of technical arts and from whom man acquires his knowledge. Again, a similar idea glimmers through the oldest tradition of Old Testament history. Cain is distinguished from Abel, the mild shepherd, as the offensive cultivator, who cannot please God. In the Genesis story of the Fall there is discoverable a remnant of an older tradition, probably a Babylonian idea, that the acquirement of knowledge is a sacrilege against divine property, severely punished by God. And even the present version of the story of the Fall emphasises that there is a limit set by God to man's knowledge.

But, above all, it is the story of the Tower of Babel which is most significant for our problem. Men have united in order to make a name for themselves, they want to build a city to keep them together and make them powerful, they want to build a tower whose top " may reach unto heaven ". But God steps in and prevents them from perfecting their tower by confounding their language. In this stupendous symbol of timeless validity a number of elements are united. The creative power and activity of man, represented by architecture, at one and the same time expresses his will to make a name for himself, to acquire fame, and also his unsuccessful attempt to keep human society together by co-operative action. In the third place, and most significantly, this creative ability expresses man's tendency to withdraw himself from the divine power and to exalt himself into the divine heights.

It would, however, be one-sided and even false if we thought that this was all that the Bible has to say about the creativity of man. As a matter of fact, the Bible reckons quite naturally with this cultural or civilising capacity and activity of man, but without placing any specific accent on it. These creative powers are gifts of God and therefore good. Only their misuse is bad. I think it is legitimate to interpret the parable of the talents (from which our use of the word talent comes) as meaning that man is responsible before God for this as well as for all other gifts which he has received from his Creator, and that he is bound to use them in such a way that the Lord can acknowledge the service of the servant as faithful. But it is true that the interest of the Bible, in the New Testament as well as in the Old Testament, never dwells on these creative elements as such, but is entirely directed to the central motive of all this and any other natural activity: " Whether therefore ye eat, or drink, or what-soever ye do, do all to the glory of God ".[93]

It is difficult to say whether this motive of the subordination of all human activity to the honour of God has been stimulating or has had the opposite effect within the sphere of Western humanity. But there cannot be the least doubt that this motivation has been a *directing* force of creativity in the highest degree. The history of culture in the early Christian, in the mediæval, in the Reformation and post-Reformation times is one great proof of that thesis. All cultural activity, art and science, music and poetry, applied arts, as well as social institutions, the state, the law, the organisation of economic life, customs of civic life, in short everything capable of carrying the imprint of the human mind, has been brought, at least theoretically and symbolically, under this highest category: *deo gloria, deo servitium.* It is true that this *deo gloria* was understood all too often in a narrow, clerical or ecclesiastical sense, and that for centuries the Virgin or the angels and the saints overshadowed God's glory. But within these limitations the European life of these twelve or thirteen centuries, from Constantine to the time of the Enlightenment, is the great example of a civilisation which is dominated by the idea that all human creativity and action ought to be a service of God.

Now, this positive relation between faith and culture is not the only one. There is also the phenomenon of Anchoritism with its radical denial of culture or civilised life. There is the monastic movement which, particularly in its several initial phases, was highly critical of culture, even to the extent of radical denial. There are also the different sectarian movements that show a tendency toward withdrawal from the complexities of the cultural life into the so-called " simple life ". There is Puritanism with its distinctively narrow cultural interest and its mistrust of many forms of art and cultural life. There is the pietistic movement with its semi-ascetic outlook. Furthermore, one cannot deny that in all these movements there is expressing itself a genuinely Christian motive, a critical standing aloof from an all too optimistic identification of the spiritual and the cultural. This critical line must certainly be included in any discussion of the relation between Christian faith and cultural activity. But two things must be observed.

First, in most of these movements we can discover, apart from Christian faith, another religious force which is primarily responsible for this negative attitude, namely Neoplatonic mysticism, within which there is inherent a dualistic metaphysics that has ascetism as its practical outgrowth. Second, we should not deny that apart from the Anchorite movement, which can hardly be called genuinely Christian, all the other movements, whilst critical in some parts, are most positive with regard to some other features of human civilisation. We should not forget what the Benedictines have done for the transmission of the heritage of ancient classical culture. We cannot pass over the magnificent architecture of one of the most radical and austere monastic movements, that of Cluny. We have to acknowledge with the highest praise the humanistic and scientific zeal of Puritanism, the dignified style of middle-class architecture within the Moravian community, and so forth.

Furthermore, in this connection it is necessary to reject the wide-spread misunderstanding with regard to the cultural effects of the Reformation. Certainly the iconoclasm which resulted in some parts of the world from Reformation preaching, and the abolition of the cult of the Virgin and the saints, have to a considerable extent narrowed the range of ecclesiastical art.

The Reformation and the Puritan movements must not, however, be identified. Neither is the intensity of a Christian culture to be measured by the extent of art employed in the service of the organised Church. We should never forget that it was within the realm of the early Lutheran Church that one of the greatest cultural creations took place in the shape of German church music, from Martin Luther to Johann Sebastian Bach, and that it was on the soil of Calvinistic Holland that a development of painting took place, equal to that of the Italian Renaissance, and reaching in Rembrandt one of those highest pinnacles of art where only a few names are inscribed. Furthermore, it should not be forgotten that Rembrandt is a painter who increasingly made the interpretation of Biblical history his main artistic endeavour, just as Bach throughout his life had put his incomparable musical genius in the service of the divine

Word and often expressed his conception of music as being nothing but an attempt of man to glorify God.

These examples of creativity being subordinated to a truly Christian view of life in the post-Reformation era have their parallels in other fields: in poetry, in natural science, in scholarship, not forgetting the economic and political spheres. Names like those of Johannes Kepler, Hugo Grotius, John Milton, William the Silent of Orange, and, above all, the large share of Calvinistic theology in the formation of democratic institutions may be sufficient to prove that, where Luther's and Calvin's interpretation of the Christian message had been accepted in living faith, the creative mind never felt itself hampered, but rather directed and even stimulated by that faith.

It can easily be understood that the progressive emancipation from Christianity which took place in the modern world also expressed itself in a different evaluation of creativity. We can trace this new temper back to the Renaissance. From then onwards the bright light of fame is directed on the creative individual as never before. Let us not forget that creativity is something relative and differential; even the average man has a certain measure of creativity, modest as it may be; every one gives his personal stamp to his life, his surroundings, to his house. Creativity ranges from a minimum to a maximum. This maximum we call genius. While in the time when creativity was subordinated to the religious meaning of life this difference was not accentuated and even the highest genius remained anonymous, now this differential character of creativity becomes important, and the creative talent or genius sees to it that the artificer's name is connected with his work. The epoch of fame is beginning; or, to be more exact, the epoch in which fame is not reserved for great generals and statesmen, but becomes something taken for granted within the spheres of art, science and scholarship. It is the time when Vasari writes his lexicon of famous painters.

In that, as in many other respects, the Renaissance is indeed a renascence of Greco-Roman antiquity. We have seen already, in previous connections, how important a rôle the fame of the creative genius plays in the development of the idea of personality. But there is still a difference. In Greece the creative individual remained in the first place a member of his people, a citizen of his *polis*. With the beginning of the modern era the meaning of individual fame becomes different. The 1500 years of Christian history had produced a sense of individual personality unknown to antiquity. The individual has an eternal destiny as an individual. This Christian personalism lies between antiquity and the modern epoch. But since the Renaissance a thoroughgoing transformation has taken place. It is no longer man as such, but it is the creative individual upon whom this supreme accent is placed. The creative individual steps out of the general crowd and is illuminated by a spotlight of hitherto unparalleled intensity. The names of the great masters are spread abroad over the whole world and their fame is cherished with the greatest solicitude. In the realm of liberal art, but even more in that of science, the rivalry of great men is the order of the day, not seldom taking the ugly form of disputes about priority. To be a man, a human being, is something; but to be a famous, eminent, creative man is much more.

This is only one aspect of the rising importance attached to creativity. More and more the creative element becomes the supreme criterion of that which characterises man as man, the human as human. The development of the creative individuality becomes the guiding principle of education. Rousseau's Emile is educated in solitude in order to preserve his original individuality and to keep it from being spoiled by the conventionalities of society. Originality, elemental primitivity, individuality *à tout prix* becomes the slogan. The hero worship of great individuals becomes a feature of our modern life. As mediæval man made his pilgrimage to some sacred place where the bones of a saint were buried, modern man makes his pilgrimage to the spot where the great poets or scientists lived or died; mausoleums of great geniuses are built where everything concerning that person, his life and activity can be seen. The biographical material concerning the great poets, musicians, thinkers, artists, becomes immense. The smallest detail of the life of Goethe is piously registered and preserved. It is particularly in the epoch of Romanticism that the veneration of genius reaches its maximum. According to Schelling, it is the creative mind, the work of the genius, in which the divine creativity of nature, identical with God-head, reaches its culminating point. In the creative work of the genius "the holy, eternally-creating divine power of the world which engenders all things"[94] breaks forth. Creative genius is the highest manifestation of creative deity. The man of genius, so we read in the book of a late Romantic philosopher, is a happy solution of the tragedy of human history.[95] Genius is the manifestation of the world-spirit. "Music is a higher revelation than all wisdom and philosophy," says Beethoven.

Whilst this metaphysical interpretation of genius has become rare in our days, we are certainly affected by that change within the hierarchy of values according to which human creativity, talent and genius takes the highest place and is the measure and criterion of human value. The man of genius may do what he likes, whatever seems necessary to his productive work; genius is an excuse for everything. To apply moral standards to the man of genius appears as a sign of the narrowmindedness of commonplace people. For the creative genius there exists a special decalogue, the first commandment of which is: I am creative, therefore I can do what I find good. Here we have a kind of Nietzschean power-morality. Morality may be good for the large masses, but for the great, exceptional man it has no validity. As a matter of fact, Nietzsche's aristocratic doctrine of the superman has its origin just as much in this Romantic veneration of genius as in a naturalistic conception of political power. One merges into the other, one helps the other. But it is not morality alone which is devaluated, but also religion. One who is himself a god needs no religion; he is divine in himself. He must not bow his head. Creativity takes the place of the religious element. Is it not this which is expressed in Goethe's sentence: "Wer Wissenschaft und Kunst besitzt, der hat Religion; wer sie nicht besitzt, der habe Religion?" The creative spirit is a substitute for religion as well as for morality. Productivity becomes in itself the meaning and principle of life.

This shift in the order of values could not fail to produce fatal results. I would recall here what we said earlier, that culture viewed from the standpoint of creativity, as well as creativity itself, is primarily a formal phenomenon. Creativity, as such, is indifferent to content; it can manifest itself in any content. If the work is original, creative, a work of genius, its content is unimportant. The famous pear of Manet is first-class painting just as much as Michelangelo's frescoes in the Sistine. Creative genius can manifest itself just as well in a ballet-dancer of Degas as in Rembrandt's engravings on the parable of the prodigal son. Incontestable as this is, this dissociation of the creative element from content indicates a fatal development. Creativity which follows its own logic of formalism, and therefore despises any reference to content, more and more loses content and becomes a trifling formalism. Certainly we believe in the full artistic earnestness of Manet painting his pear or of Goya painting his famous piece of raw meat. Both are works of the first rank, filling everyone who is sensitive to painting with delight and admiration; and yet everyone who has not succumbed to the cult of genius, in enjoying these masterpieces will be worried by the question: Where does this lead; must not this kind of art end in purest abstraction, in lifeless formalism?

This is not the only indication of coming decay. Once the belief is established that productivity is the meaning of human life, none can prevent this point of view being transferred to the lower regions of human production, especially since it is only a minority of people who are capable of taking part actively or receptively in art and science, at least in the sense of a passionate interest or a total self-abandonment. The slogan of productivity being the true meaning of life directs the large majority of men to another field, a field of production which is in closer connection with every-day exigencies and interests, namely the field of mechanical or technical invention in the service of economic production.

It corresponds to a materialist, quantitative conception of life, by which the technical inventor becomes the adored symbol of creativity, and new machinery the measure of progress. Edison is thought of as the greatest of creative minds. It is in this sphere of technical invention that man enters, so to speak, into human competition with the Creator of nature. By architecture and technics he produces a man-made world, an artificial nature, somehow re-surfacing and effectively hiding nature. It is here that the motive of the Tower of Babel story is most apparent. Man-creator, competitor of God-creator. Certainly technics and building are first of all very matter-of-fact useful things. The multi-millionaire building titanic skyscrapers is, as a rule, no romantic but a realist who calculates exactly how much this building is going to bring in in dollars and cents. Furthermore, his skyscraper is a form of architecture produced by the high cost of city property and the scarcity of space. But, all the same, it is in these architectural structures that something of that dangerous titanism finds expression, which the narrative of the Tower of Babel has in mind. It is, perhaps, not so much the builders as individuals, but the generation which sees these colossi rise from the ground and sees also the greatest rivers bridged, the Atlantic ocean crossed in a day's flight and the city of Hiroshima destroyed by a single bomb—it is this generation which is tempted with a feeling of God-like power.

No doubt, in all that man does he is fundamentally and in many ways dependent on the work of the Divine Creator. It is from nature that he gets his material and often also, without knowing it, the guiding ideas of his production. He can never free himself from the laws of statics and dynamics, but has to adapt himself to them. However, there is a great temptation to forget in the case of his own creations his dependence on that which God creates and to feel himself in his creativity as creator of his own existence. "Man is free only if he owes his existence to himself," we heard Karl Marx saying. The more man lives in his artificial man-made reality amongst man's structures and machinery, the more strongly he receives the impression that he is the creator of his own existence. It is no accident that this is the statement of Karl Marx, *i.e.* of a man who saw man only as an economic producer.

This does not mean that technics or productivity inevitably estrange man from God. Even the most creative mind, and even the man who has to live entirely among machinery and within a man-made surrounding, *can* remain God-conscious and *can* do whatever he does for the glory of God. Human creativity and the man-made reality is not the reason or cause, but it is the great temptation to Godlessness. The more creative man is, the more he is tempted to confound himself with the Creator. The danger is the titanism of the creative man who, inebriated by his feeling of creativity and in a kind of mystic ecstasy, thinks himself to be God. It is that old phenomenon of ὕβρις, of man's forgetting his limits, which brings him to ruin.

Thus far we have been speaking of creativity as such. But the detachment from the Christian faith, as we see it taking place in the modern world, has its results also in the relation of the different spheres in which man is productive. The phenomenon we are now dealing with is the tendency to autonomy of culture and civilisation. Modern man, determined to free human civilisation from the tutelage of the Church, thinks it necessary for that purpose to emancipate it also from the predominance of the Christian revelation, and hence proclaims a programme of autonomy. This is the decisive step in the direction of secularisation, of this-worldliness. The roots of culture that lie in the transcendent sphere are cut off; culture and civilisation must have their law and meaning in themselves.

Now, what makes this problem particularly difficult is the fact that, beyond all doubt, every domain of human culture and civilisation does have its own immanent law. Every science, like mathematics, has its own principles, norms and criteria, which certainly cannot and must not be learned from divine revelation, but are immanent in the subject matter, and must be learned by entering into it. The same is true of every art, every technique, whether it be the liberal arts, the technical arts, or the arts of politics and economics. In each of these fields expert knowledge is necessary, and this expert knowledge is the same for everyone, whether Christian or non-Christian. Even the good Samaritan, who cares for the man fallen among thieves, has to do it with expert knowledge that does not come from Christian love, but from practical experience. Faith and love do not make expert knowledge superfluous. In the good Samaritan they worked together without any conflict. It is love which is the inspiration of expert activity. There is a technique of good Samaritanship which he who earnestly loves wants to learn and to apply. The principle, then, of the autonomy of the sciences and arts is based on truth. But it is only half the truth.

It is no longer a half truth but a fatal error if such an autonomy is understood to mean something that stands upon itself and calls for no subordination, no fitting into a higher unity. The best Samaritan-technique is no use if love, the will to help, does not move man to use it. The detachment of culture from Christianity produced the fatally erroneous belief that culture or creativity needs no subordination to a higher unit, but can live on its own resources. The vehemence with which the so-called Christian tutelage of culture is rejected is not incomprehensible, considering how intolerably in past centuries Christianity has fettered culture. This is particularly obvious in the field of science. The narrow borderlines in which Church dogma kept scientific endeavour hampered scientific development for centuries. No wonder that the liberation of science from this theological tutelage took place in a violent manner, revealing a deep resentment which lingers on to the present day. It was philosophy that led the way and cut the ice; the sciences, the arts, developments in economic and political thought followed. The tendency is the same everywhere: freedom from ecclesiastical, theological and Christian presuppositions—autonomy!

This postulate of autonomy in its unconditional sense does not take account of a most important fact, namely the unity of human life. There is a totalitarian character in the questions, what for? what is the meaning? Meaning, as we have seen in a previous lecture, is totality. All domains of human life must be brought into the unity of meaning in order to be meaningful. This unity of meaning does not lie in any one of them as such; the unity of meaning lies only in that principle in which the

totality of man and nature is grounded, *i.e.* the divine will.   In
the first centuries of the modern age the spiritual leaders still
knew that; they did not want to emancipate civilisation from
God, but only from the Church and also from the specifically
Christian form of religion.   They did not want to abandon
theology as the basis of civilisation, but they were seeking a
rational or natural theology.   It was only in the course of time
that it became clear that such a natural theology, offering a solid
basis apart from Christian revelation, does not exist.   Each
philosophical school produced its own " rational theology ", and
the metaphysical chaos finally became so great that the quest for
a theological basis was deserted altogether.   It was then that the
programme of the autonomy of civilisation was understood in a
radical, in an entirely secular sense.   What was the consequence?

First, that the different domains fell asunder.   The new age
experienced the departmentalisation of cultural life.   Science
developed itself independently alongside art; so did the arts,
economic life and the state.   The programme involved in the
autonomy of civilisation produced a necessarily disconnected
specialisation.   But this was only the outward appearance of a
more fundamental change: each domain gradually lost its
meaning.   According to the postulate of autonomy, the meaning
of science, of art, of economics, of politics was sought, each in
itself alone.   But meaning being totality, the postulate of autonomy had resulted in each one of these domains trying to be the
totality in itself.   It is in this manner that the different " isms "
were created: " intellectualism " as the scientific totalitarianism,
" æstheticism " as the totalitarianism of art, " economism ", and
finally political totalitarianism, as the most dangerous of all
these.

Intellectualism and æstheticism still have a spiritual heritage
and basis.   Intellectualism is based on the total claim of science.
Now, since science is a great spiritual good, the fatal consequences
of its false autonomy, of the totalitarianism of science, do not
appear so quickly.   On the other hand, science is the domain in
which specialisation proceeds most rapidly.   With its tremendous specialisation during recent centuries, it became difficult to

see a meaning in any one of these sciences. Furthermore, scientific activity is based so entirely on one of our spiritual functions only, namely intelligence, that the progressive impoverishment and deformation of the human soul could not but appear most drastically. And, finally, it became clear in the progress of science that science, as such, is incapable of giving life a meaning. For science never declares what ought to be, but only what is. Science only describes and explains facts, it has no access to meaning.

Æstheticism in many ways had a better chance, for art has such a manifold claim on the mind and soul of man, and it can move the depth of his heart in such a measure that the destructive effect of its totalitarian claim does not easily appear. Art has never undergone such a process of specialisation as science. But æstheticism produced evils of its own. First of all, only a small minority of people were capable of believing that art could be the meaning of life, because the world of art is so detached from the problems of practical everyday affairs. Furthermore, the more art proclaimed its autonomy in the principle " art for art's sake " and so detached itself from the rest of life, the more empty it became. The separation of content and form, which was the necessary result of this autonomy, could not but manifest itself in an extreme formalism, and therefore a progressive impoverishment. Finally, æstheticism as a philosophy of life inevitably leads to moral and social anarchy and chaos. Is not this one of the roots of the weakness of France, that country which more than any other was inclined to follow the doctrines of æstheticism?

Much more obvious and brutal is the effect of totalitarianism in the range of economics and politics. The emancipation of economic life led to that typical release of the economic motive which is so characteristic of the Western world in the 19th and 20th centuries, particularly in the countries with a predominantly Germanic and Anglo-Saxon population. It is not only the mentality which we are wont to connect with the capitalistic system [96] and with " Manchester liberalism ", but also the reaction against it in Marxian pan-economism, which is a clear manifestation of this evolution. Marxism and capitalism are twin brothers, children of the same economic totalitarianism which, having got hold of Western man within recent generations, has so deeply damaged, brutalised and impoverished Western society. The devastations of the soul and the deformity of human life produced by capitalist and Marxist pan-economism are indescribable.

Still, they are surpassed by what political totalitarianism has done to us since the formation of totalitarian states began in 1917. What we nowadays call totalitarianism is but *one* of the forms of the totalitarian principle. It is the application of this principle to the state and to politics. It is necessary to see political totalitarianism in this larger context. It is *one* of the inevitable products of the principle of autonomy. But it is also the one in which the falsehood of that principle becomes most manifest. It is even more dangerous than all the other totalitarianisms, because of an element connected with it alone, the element of compulsion. The æsthete, seeing the meaning of life in art, does that on his own account; he can force no one else to share his error. The totalitarian state, however, possesses both the will and the power to force everyone to live as if the state were the meaning of life, as if the state had that all-importance which belongs to God alone. But when we think of this monster, the totalitarian state, we should never forget whose child it is: it is the product of that programme of autonomy which was formulated as a consequence of the attempt to emancipate culture from Christian faith. If this principle of autonomy and totality is taken up by the state, that state at once claims—and claims effectively—the monopoly of totalitarianism. The totalitarian state does away with those rival pseudo-religions, intellectualism and æstheticism, just as it tries to do away with its most dangerous rival, true religion, in order to establish itself as the only acknowledged and effective religion, the pseudo-religion of political totalitarianism. The economic element, however, even a totalitarian *economism*, it incorporates in itself, creating the conditions which you may call totalitarian state-socialism or state-capitalism, as you please. And this is the end not only of freedom and humanity, but also of all true creativity. For spiritual creativity and collectivist tyranny are mutually exclusive.

Man cannot tear out of his life that unity which is in God alone without the gravest consequences. If he does so, the consequence is the proclamation of autonomy and the totalitarianism of the different domains. But in the competition between these different totalitarianisms the political makes a prey of all the others, because it alone has the power of coercion, the power to prohibit and to annihilate what it does not like. It replaces arguments and the free competition of spiritual forces by machine-guns and concentration camps. In such a fashion it destroys all creative life, the brutal automaton of power triumphing over the creative spirit.

Let us once more come back to the creative man as he is seen within the Christian faith. God, the Creator, having created man in His image, has given him creative powers; where man acknowledges his Creator, he knows that he cannot create from nothing as God does, that therefore his human creativity is a mere imitation of God's, taking place within the limits and according to the laws and dependent upon the materials which God gives. Where God is acknowledged as the Creator, man knows that the ultimate meaning of His creatures is the same as the meaning of all life: the glory of God and the service of men. If he remains within this boundary every domain of human activity keeps its own rights and its own kind. Moreover, each one then keeps within its limits. This is particularly true, and particularly important, in regard to the most dangerous of them all, the state, which is then placed under the control of the divine law and kept within the limits of its functions. The state is thus only a servant and not a master of human life. Its so-called sovereignty is strictly limited by the God-given purpose of the state, and the " sovereignty " of the individual states is limited by the equal rights of every other " sovereign " state. That is to say, the dangerous principle of sovereignty is limited by the sovereignty of God, both internally and externally, and thereby a due relation is maintained.

Where the principle of autonomy is substituted for faith in the Creator, this unity and order in human life fall to pieces, and finally the state, as the substituted unifier, usurps the rights of all and plays the rôle of God on earth. It can do so more effectively when it is combined with pan-economism and technocracy. It is then that man, identifying himself with that state, can believe himself to be God, the creator of his own existence, having in his hands unlimited powers and illimitable authority over other men. This totalitarian man is, in all probability, the monster of the Apocalypse who tramples down and devours humanity. And the totalitarian state is the most urgent problem of our civilisation at this present hour.

For it is precisely in this present generation that it should become obvious where the de-Christianisation of culture and civilisation—the main feature of the past few centuries—leads. Humanity therefore is facing in our time, as at no time before, this alternative: *either* to continue along this road of the modern age, the road of emancipation from the Christian truth which leads to the total effacement of anything truly human and perhaps even to its complete physical annihilation; *or* to go back to the source of justice, truth and love, which is the God of justice, truth and love in whom only lies the power of salvation.

NOTES AND REFERENCES

[1] Oswald Spengler, *The Decline of the West*.

[2] Jakob Burckhardt, *Briefe an Preen* (24.7.1889).

[3] Huyzinga, *Im Schatten von morgen*.

[4] Of course there has remained in many of the European countries a good deal of Christian tradition as well as a considerable stock of truly idealist thought. But the main trend was in the opposite direction.

[5] *Cf.* John Baillie, Riddell Lectures, 1945, *What is Christian Civilisation?* to which I am greatly indebted.

[6] Albert Schweizer, *Geschichte der Leben-Jesu—Forschung*.

[7] Even if we give more weight to the ancient traditions about Plato's connections with the wisdom of the Orient than has been customary in recent times, as J. Bidez has pleaded for in his Gifford Lectures (*Eos ou Platon et l'orient*, 1945), we can see no trace of any influence from the side of Hebrew prophetic sources. Whether this would also be true with regard to Hellenistic philosophy before Philo, *e.g.* Posidonius, may be regarded as an open question.

[8] *Cf.* Hegel's philosophy of history. One might contend that Max Weber's *Religionssoziologie* inaugurated a new and most fruitful line holding a *juste milieu* between the two extremes or rather doing justice to both the material as well as the spiritual realities. But, so far, Max Weber's *Religionssoziologie* has not had the following it deserves either in his own or other countries.

[9] The purpose of this lecture is, as the reader will have noticed, different from that of a number of Gifford Lecturers such as Laird (*Theism and Cosmology*, 1939), Bradley (*Ideals of Religion*, 1907, published 1940), J. Ward (*The Realm of Ends*, 1911), who deal with similar problems but from a purely philosophical standpoint. My first and supreme aim here is not to prove philosophically the truth of the Christian idea of Being but to show how different it is from all philosophical conceptions and what its implications are.

[10] *Cf.* Emil Brunner, *Die christliche Lehre von Gott*, Dogmatik Bd. I, particularly *Erster Abschnitt, Das Wesen Gottes und seine Eigenschaften*. The opposite view and tendency is prevalent in most Roman Catholic writers, as set forth with particular learning and clarity in E. Gilson's Gifford Lectures, *L'esprit de la philosophie mediévale*.

159

[11] Before the philosopher criticises the Christian idea of creation he ought to see and acknowledge the unbridgeable gulf which separates it from its more or less monistic alternatives—a postulate which is certainly not fulfilled by the treatment which Laird (*Theism and Cosmology*, pp. 118 ff.) gives to it.

[12] For a thorough treatment of the idea of contingency from the point of view of a philosopher who tries to do full justice to Christian thought, see HEINRICH BARTH, *Philosophie der Erscheinung*, 1. *Teil*, *Altertum und Mittelalter*, pp. 326 ff., particularly pp. 355 ff., where he develops this idea in its most Christian form as set forth by Petrus Damiani.

[13] *Cf.* F. A. LANGE, *Geschichte des Materialismus*, Vol. II, p. 196.

[14] *Cf.* the book of the famous mathematician, H. WEYLL of Princeton, *The Open Universe*.

[15] Psalm XXXVI.

[16] In the discussions about this lecture I was asked whether I was not taking here the line of Berkeley's idealist philosophy. My answer is : certainly not. First, what I have said is not a result of philosophical reflection but an exposition of Christian faith. Second, according to the Christian faith in God the Creator and in the creation of the world, the reality of this created world is firmly asserted, even if it is said that this reality is God's thought and the product of His will. God's will—as distinguished from God's ideas—does not enter Berkeley's argument at all.

[17] KARL BARTH, *Kirchliche Dogmatik*, III. Bd., 1. Teil, S. 5 und 27.

[18] *Cf.* for instance, the sceptical philosophy of Sextus Empiricus.

[19] FEUERBACH, *Vorlesungen über das Wesen der Religion*, ed. Jodl, S. 21.

[20] It is necessary here to refer to a writer who, so far, is entirely unknown in English-speaking countries and who shares with Martin Buber the merit of having discovered the I-Thou relation : FERDINAND EBNER, in his work *Das Wort und die geistigen Realitäten*, 1921. Martin Buber seems to have made his discovery independently of Ebner although a little later, *Ich und Du*, 1923. As the third writer to whom we owe much for the understanding of the Thou-I relation I should mention Friedrich Gogarten, who later on unfortunately developed an ethics of authority which led to misuse by certain propagators of Nazi ideology. Eberhard Grisebach in his earlier works belongs to the same group, whilst Martin Heidegger, outstanding as a philosopher and as founder of what is called the school of existentialism, is only slightly related to the I-Thou philosophy. All these thinkers have come under the influence of Sören Kierkegaard who might be called the founder of a Christian philosophy of " existence ".

[21] Whilst this mentality is at present more manifest in Soviet Russia than anywhere else, it is in the making in other highly industrialised countries as well. It is a product of the modern age at large, and cannot but become predominant if it is not counteracted by a strong Christian movement.

[22] It will have to be worked out in another context what the distinction of God-knowledge and world-knowledge means within the different sciences. Distinction in no way means separation. Absolute and relative knowledge are correlative.

[23] " Sonnenklarer Bericht an das grössere Publikum über das eigentliche Wesen der neuesten Philosophie, ein Versuch, die Leser zum Verstehen zu zwingen ", 1801, sämtl. Wke., II, S. 324-420.

[24] i Cor. VIII, 2, 3.

[25] John XIV, 6.

[26] *Cf.* Brunner, *The Divine-Human Encounter* (*Wahrheit als Begegnung*) and *Revelation and Reason*, chapter 2.

[27] *Cf.* Plato's *Phaedo*, the description of the monk-like disposition of the real philosopher, 66-7.

[28] *Cf.* Plato's idea of the good, *Republic*, VI, 508, and its modern parallel, Kant's idea of God as being the principle of practical reason.

[29] Of course Bergson's idea of *durée réelle* was an attempt to overcome this spatialisation of time ; just as, in a very different way, was Heidegger's conception of *Dasein* (*Sein und Zeit*). But both solutions of the time problem are very different from that of Christianity, Bergson's *durée* being a pantheistic or mystical mixture of temporality and eternity, Heidegger's *Dasein*, on the other hand, being correlative to life-unto-death, without a Beyond. But it is highly important that the leading philosophers of our age are dealing with the problem of time much more intensively than any previous school of philosophy.

[30] James I, 17.

[31] Gal. IV, 4.

[32] Eph. I, 9.

[33] *Cf.* my article, " Das Einmalige und der Existenzcharakter ", in *Deutsche Blätter für Philosophie*, 1929 ; and *Die christliche Lehre von Gott*, S. 285 ff.

[34] Matth. XXV, 12.

[35] Of course it is true that Augustine's *De Civitate Dei* is no *philosophy* of history as Troeltsch points out (*Der Historismus und seine Probleme*, S. 14 and note, S. 15). The question is whether anything which Troeltsch would have acknowledged as *philosophy* would be able to deal with that what a Christian would acknowledge as *history*.

[36] Rom. VIII, 38.

[37] Rom. VIII, 18.

[38] Matt. XIII, 30.

[39] The first idealist philosophy of history is Lessing's *Erziehung des Menschengeschlechts*, 1777 and 1780, soon followed by Herder's *Ideen zur Philosophie der Geschichte der Menschheit*, 1784-90. I do not know any system of philosophy of history, not even Hegel's, which shows more clearly the traits of this optimistic evolutionism than Schleiermacher's, embedded in his " philosophische Ethik ".

[40] The typical and most influential representative of this optimistic evolutionism is Auguste Comte in his *Cours de Philosophie Positive* and *Système de Politique Positive, ou traité de sociologie, instituant la religion de l'humanité, 1830-54*. Whilst in Comte's system the faith in science is combined with a spiritual, although entirely immanent element, Herbert Spencer s evolutionist philosophy has got rid even of this remainder of religion or idealism. Spencer puts his faith in evolution entirely on the natural process of " differentiation " and " integration " and on the rôle of utilitarian thinking. The more recent idea of " emergent evolution " —as, *e.g.* expounded in Laird's Gifford Lectures (*Theism and Cosmology*) is a combination of speculative idealism and naturalistic evolutionism following Bergson's neo-Schelingian idea of *évolution créatrice*.

[41] *Cf.* the article " Logos " in Kittel's *Theologisches Wörterbuch zum Neuen Testament*, B., *Der Logos in Griechentum und Hellenismus*, IV, 76-89.

[42] The above cited article " Logos " in Kittel's *Wörterbuch* shows clearly both the unity and the differences of the Greek philosophical schools, as well as the fundamental difference between all of them and the Biblical idea of " the word of God ".

[43] *Cf.* Bousset, *Die Religion des Judentums*, S. 506-520.

[44] *Cf.* Delvaille, *Essai sur l'idée du progrès jusqu'a la fin du 18me siècle.*.

[45] Leibnitz has often been named among the originators of the idea of universal progress. Quite wrongly so. His view of the future is rather pessimistic. There is in his *Nouveaux essais* a passage which ranks him with those prophets of future European chaos named in our first lecture. I cannot refrain from quoting it in full. Speaking of the disciples of rationalist philosophers he says : " Qui se croyant déchargés de l'importunée crainte d'une providence surveillante et d'un avenir menaçant, lachent la bride à leurs passions brutales, et tournent leur esprit à séduir et à corrompre les autres ; et s'ils sont ambitieux et d'un naturel un peu dur, ils seront capables pour leur plaisir ou avancement de mettre le feu aux quatre coins de la terre. . . . Je trouve même que les opinions approchantes s'insinuant peu à peu dans l'esprit des hommes du grand monde

qui règlent les autres et dont dépendent les affaires et se glissant dans les livres à la mode *disposent toutes choses à la revolution générale dont l'Europe est menacée et achèvent de détruire* ce qui reste encore dans le monde de sentiments généreux. . . . Ces public spirits, comme les Anglais les appellent, diminuent extrèmement et ne sont plus à la mode ; et ils cesseront d'avantage quand ils cesseront à être soutenu par la bonne Morale et la vraie Religion. . . . Et si pour la grandeur ou par caprice quelqu'un versait *un déluge de sang, s'il renversait tout en dessus dessous on compterait cela pour rien.* . . . Si l'on se corrige encore de cette *maladie d'esprit épidemique* dont les mauvais effets commencent à être visibles, ces maux, peut-être, seront prévenus ; mais si elle va croissant *la providence corrigera les hommes par la révolution* même qui en doit naître." (Leibnitz : *Op. philosoph.*, ed. Erdmann, p. 387.) In another place he says : " The atheist and earthly mind propagates itself in such a manner that one has reason to believe that the world is already in its old age. The last sect in Christendom and in general in the world will be atheism " (quoted—with a wrong reference—in E. de Rougemont, *Les deux cités*, II, p. 109).

⁴⁶ It is one of the most deep-seated differences between Britain and the European continent that in English idealistic philosophy the connection with the Christian tradition was never cut, whilst on the continent, and particularly in German idealism (since Fichte), it was. If ever a history of the Gifford Lectures should be written, this fact would come to the light most strikingly. On the continent, philosophy got increasingly out of touch with theology (whilst the reverse would not be true during the 19th century !) ; in Great Britain the tie was never completely broken. Therefore idealism always was somehow " Christian idealism ", even there where it was not conscious of it or would not have been willing to admit it. What is said above is said with regard to the continental situation. This difference accounts for many things of which not the least is the immunity of Great Britain from totalitarianism.

⁴⁷ John 1, 18.

⁴⁸ John 1, 17.

⁴⁹ Gal. v, 6.

⁵⁰ I am referring to the so-called existentialist philosophy, both of Heidegger and of Sartre.

⁵¹ Otto's famous book, *The Idea of the Holy*, is misleading in so far as it describes a phenomenon of holiness as being a general phenomenon of religion whilst it is—not in all, but in some of its most important features—a specifically Biblical (particularly an Old Testament) phenomenon.

⁵² For this sketch of Christian anthropology *cf.* my book, *Der*

Mensch im Widerspruch, 1937 (*Man in Revolt*, 1939), where the implications of the idea of God-image as well as its limitations by the reality of sin are fully dealt with.

[53] So far as I know, the two historical movements have never yet been understood from this anthropological angle. The nearest approach is still Dilthey's *Weltanschauung und Analyse des Menschen seit der Renaissance, Ges. Schriften*, Bd. II), but with far more interest and understanding for the Renaissance than for the Reformation.

[54] KANT, *Kritik der reinen Vernunft, Vorrede zur zweiten Ausgabe*.

[55] EDDINGTON, in his Gifford Lectures, *The Nature of the Physical World*, 1927, in discussing the question whether there might be other solar systems, which in themselves would be the necessary presupposition of human life, says : " I should judge that perhaps not one in a hundred millions of stars can have undergone this experience in the right stage and conditions to result in the formation of a system of planets " (p. 177).

[56] ED. FUETER, *Geschichte der exakten Naturwissenschaften in der schweizerischen Aufklärung*, S. 33.

[57] Giordano Bruno, the prophet of Copernicanism, is at the same time a fierce opponent of Christian doctrine, particularly of Calvinism. In his allegorical-philosophical treatise, *The Triumphant Beast*, he attacks the whole Christian doctrine as anthropocentric and particularistic. *Cf.* Dilthey, *op. cit.*, the essay on Giordano Bruno, pp. 297-311. But Bruno's case shows clearly enough the guilt of the contemporary church, both Roman Catholic and Calvinist.

[58] It is with these problems in mind that the new attempts to restate the Christian Anthropology have been made, by myself (*Der Mensch im Widerspruch*, Engl. *Man in Revolt*, 1937 and 1939) and Reinhold Niebuhr, in his Gifford Lectures, *Human Nature and Human Destiny*, 1941 and 1942.

[59] What is here called " hominism " is more or less what has in recent times been understood in English-speaking countries by " humanism" (*cf.*, *e.g.*, Schiller, *Humanism*, 1902 ; *Studies in Humanism*, 1907, etc).

[60] Psalm CXXXIX, 13-15.

[61] *Cf.* JAEGER, *Paideia* ; F. Wehrli, *Vom antiken Humanitätsbegriff*, 1939.

[62] About Plato's views on slavery *cf. Republic*, V, 469 ; IV, 331 ; *Leges*, VI, 776. About the individualising principle as basis of a (moderate) caste-system, *cf. Republic*, III, 415 ; IV, 433, 427.

[63] How abstract the idea of man is in (later) stoicism may be seen from Epictetus' description of the universal state of the wise ; *cf. Dialogues*, III, 22.

[64] Aristotle, *Nicomachaean Ethics*, book 8.

[65] FEUERBACH, *Vorlesungen über das Wesen der Religion*, and *Das Wesen des Christentums*. For detailed references see Brunner, *Revelation and Reason*, ch. 16. D. F. Strauss, *Der alte und der neue Glaube* (1872). For Karl Marx, see his early writings edited, together with those of Engels, in the *Historisch-kritische Gesamtausgabe* of the Marx-Engel Institut, Moskau, Frankfurt, 1927.

[66] *Cf.* systems of political theory like that of Gumplowicz, Oppenheimer, Giddings, or—with very different methods but similar results—the formalism of Kelsen.

[67] 1 Cor. III, 6 ; VI, 19.

[68] It should be remembered that the negative valuation of bodily appetites or instincts as " low " is not of Christian but of Platonic origin.

[69] There was nothing accidental about Hitler's choice of Nietzsche's works as a present for his friend Mussolini, even though he himself is hardly likely to have read much of them. But it was through mediating interpreters like Bäumler (*Nietzsche, der Philosoph und Politiker*) and Spengler, *Der Untergang des Aberdlandes Mensch und Technik, politische Schriften, Jahre der Entscheidung*—a book of which more than 100,000 copies were sold—that Nietzsche's philosophy of *Wille zur Macht* became predominant.

[70] *Cf.* Dilthey, *Das natürliche System der Geisteswissenschaften im 17. Jahrhundert, op. cit.*, pp. 90 ff.

[71] This lecture is a summary of my book, *Justice and the Social Order*, 1943, Engl. 1945.

[72] As a matter of fact the concept of natural law is already accepted by Paul : Rom. I, 26 f. ; I, 32 ; II, 14 f. ; 1 Cor. XI, 14.

[73] It is not Karl Barth who is the first opponent of natural law but Ritschl and the Ritschlian school, where the opposition to this concept is grounded in Kantian agnosticism. Further back, it is romantic historicism which, in jurisprudence, as well as in theology, opposed natural law as being " unhistorical ". If the Barthians who so valiantly fought against the Hitler state only knew a little more of the history of political thinking in Germany, they would become aware of the fact that the fight against natural law resulted in the abolition of all standards by which what the present day State sees fit to declare law might be criticised.

[74] This positivist conception of law prevails in most of those representatives of political science who base their juridical and political theory on " sociological " data. It is very unfortunate that sociology was founded as a science at a time when positivistic evolutionism had become more or less an unquestioned axiom.

It is this school of naturalist sociology which bears a large share of responsibility for the destruction of justice—in theory first, in practice as a consequence.

[75] ROUSSEAU, *Discours sur l'inégalité des hommes*, Oeuvres compl., I, 282. *Contrat Social*, p. 65. The quotations are given in Brunner, *Justice and the Social Order*, p. 42.

[76] ROUSSEAU, *Contrat Social*, book I, ch. 6.

[77] *Cf.* HANS BARTH, *Wahrheit und Ideologie*, in the chapter " Ideologie und ideologisches Bewusstsein in der Philosophie von Karl Marx ", the philosophical presuppositions of the Marxian doctrine are developed with most careful documentation from Marx' writings.

[78] *Cf.* Brunner, *Die christliche Lehre von Gott*, ch. 15.

[79] Hebr. XI, 10.

[80] Gal. III, 28.

[81] 1 Cor. VII, 21 ff.

[82] Rom. VII, 15 ff.

[83] Of course, Fichte's " Ich " is not simply the empirical Ego of man. But the very fact that he substitutes for Kant's ethics of duty his ethics of freedom shows that he is in earnest in calling the absolute reality " Ich ". *Cf.* note 90.

[84] Psalm VIII, 6.

[85] There can be no question that Luther and Calvin in their fight against Roman Catholic Pelagianism, went a long way in the direction of complete, metaphysical determinism. *Cf.* Luther's *De Servo Arbitrio*. What they were driving at, however, was a truly Biblical conception of freedom as being identical with independence of God. For a more thorough treatment of this central question of Christian anthropology see my *Man in Revolt*, chapters 5 and 11.

[86] FICHTE, *Sämtl. Wke.*, V, p. 479.

[87] MARX, *op. cit.*, III, p. 124.

[88] DONALD BRINKMANN, *Mensch und Technik*, 1946, pp. 105 ff.

[89] *Cf.* Luther's classical treatise on *The Freedom of the Christian Man*.

[90] One can see this change in the development from the transcendental idealism of Kant to the metaphysical or speculative idealism of Fichte. For Kant, freedom is correlative to duty and grounded in law ; for Fichte, law is identical with freedom. There is no other law than the one to be free. See his *System der Sittenlehre* of 1798, works IV, pp. 59 ff.

[91] John VIII, 36.

[92] 2 Cor. III, 17.

[93] 1 Cor. X, 31.

[94] SCHELLING, *Ueber das Verhältnis der bildenden Künste zur Natur*, Wke., VII, S. 293.

[95] EMIL LUCKA, *Stufen der Genialität*, S. 191.

[96] The startling theory of Max Weber that Calvinism is one of the roots of modern capitalism, sponsored by Ernst Troeltsch and widely accepted by theologians and others, has met severe criticism and is in its original form untenable. A much more cautious statement of the case is made by R. H. Tawney, *Religion and the Rise of Capitalism*. See particularly his preface to the edition of 1937, pp. xi-xiv.

INDEX